Giovanni's Last Shoe

A Historical Narrative of the
Giovanni and Rosaria di Bartolomeo Family

G. MARK BARTOLOMEO

Copyright © 2022 G. Mark Bartolomeo

All rights reserved.

No part of this book may be reproduced or transmitted in any form or by any means, electronic or mechanical, including photocopying, recording, or by any information storage and retrieval system without the written permission of the author, except for the use of brief quotations in a book review or academic work.

Editing and Production by Influunt Publishing Services, Vancouver, BC, Canada.

Print ISBN: 979-8-218-00688-4

Library of Congress Control Number: 2022940438

Dedication

This book is dedicated to Giovanni Antonio di Bartolomeo,

shoemaker b. June 24, 1858 – d. January 15, 1937

Table of Contents

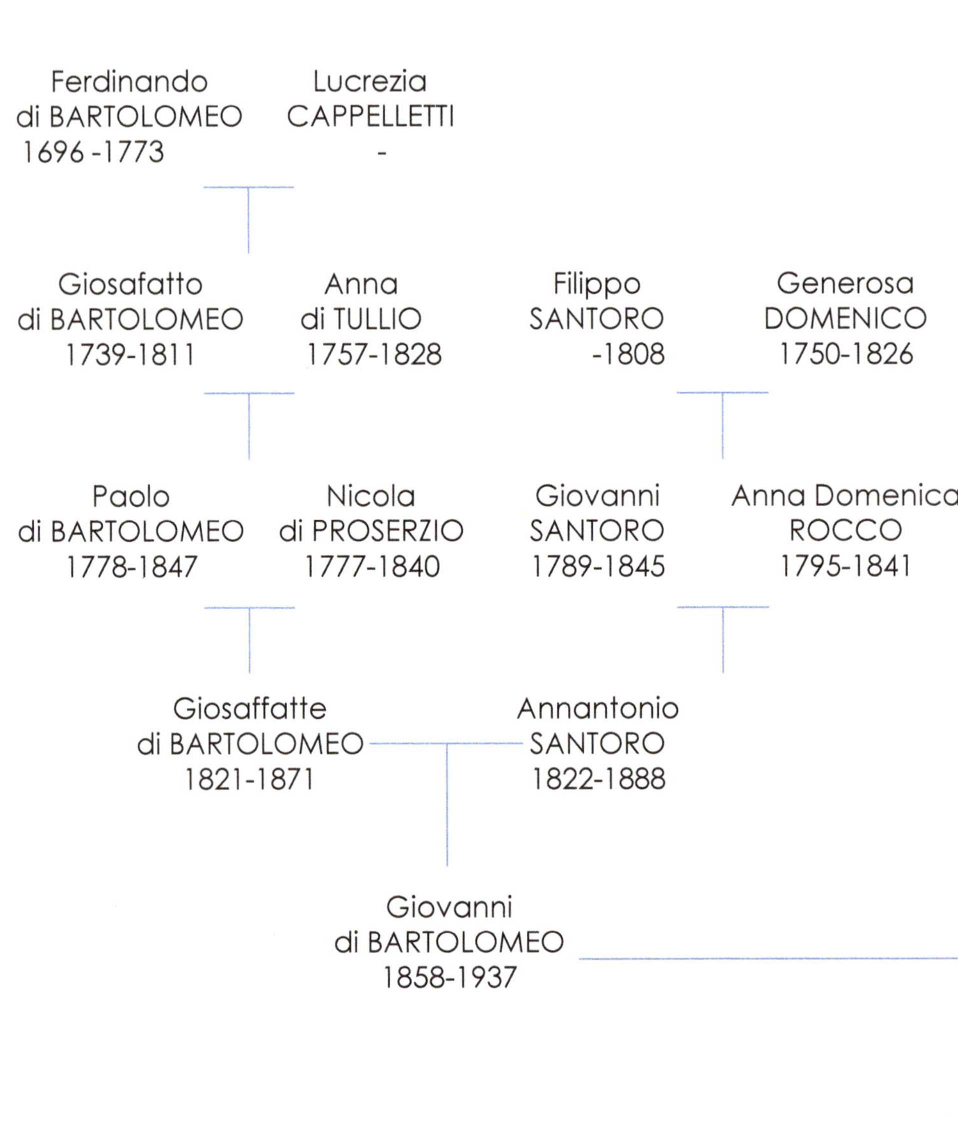
Ferdinando
di BARTOLOMEO
1696 -1773
Lucrezia
CAPPELLETTI
-
Giosafatto
di BARTOLOMEO
1739-1811
Anna
di TULLIO
1757-1828
Filippo
SANTORO
-1808
Generosa
DOMENICO
1750-1826
Paolo
di BARTOLOMEO
1778-1847
Nicola
di PROSERZIO
1777-1840
Giovanni
SANTORO
1789-1845
Anna Domenica
ROCCO
1795-1841
Giosaffatte
di BARTOLOMEO
1821-1871
Annantonio
SANTORO
1822-1888
Giovanni
di BARTOLOMEO
1858-1937
Maria
di BARTOLOMEO
1889-1954
Gaspare
di BARTOLOMEO
1892-1973
Luigi
di BARTOLOMEO
1894-1960

Giovanni & Rosaria di Bartolomeo Family Tree

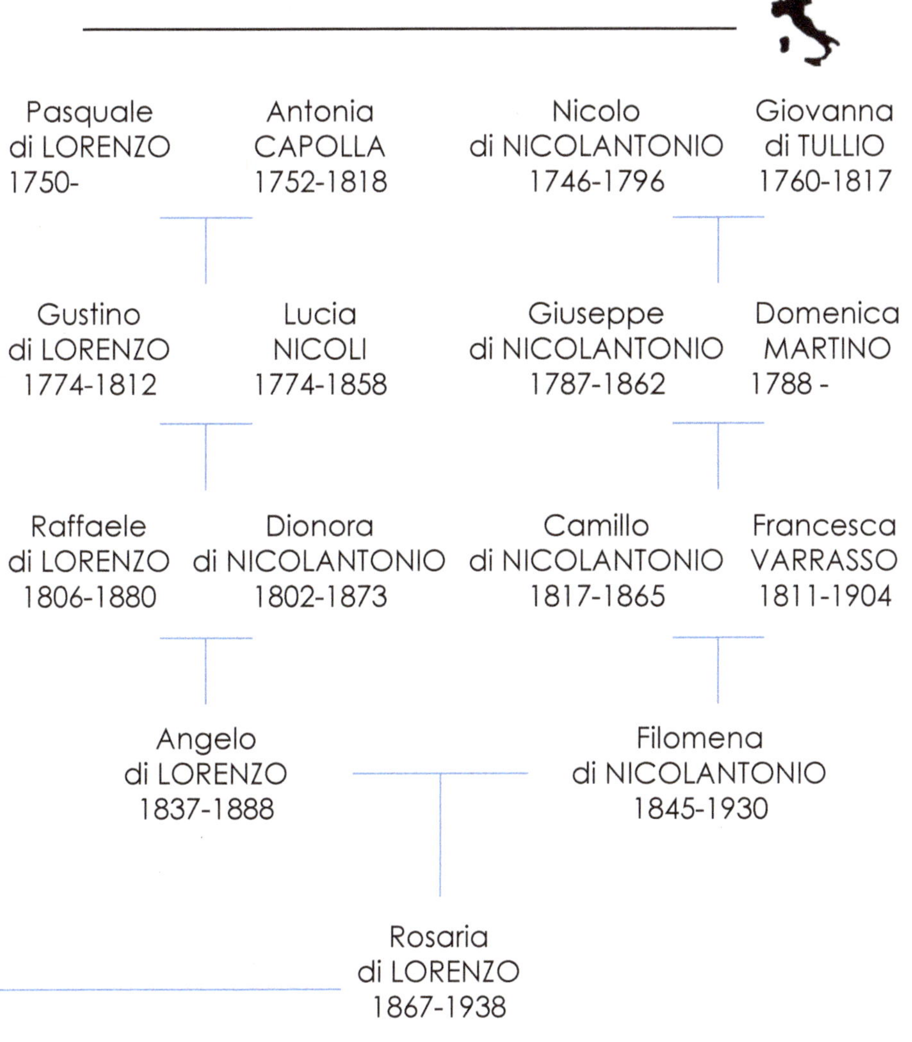

Anna di BARTOLOMEO 1897-1994	Giuseppe di BARTOLOMEO 1899-1983	Alberto di BARTOLOMEO 1900-1972	Florentina di BARTOLOMEO 1908-1991

"Children rarely want to know who their parents were before they were parents, and when age finally stirs their curiosity, there is no parent left to tell them."

—— **Russell Baker**

di Bartolomeo Family

Left to right: Anna, Alberto, Maria (standing), Rosaria, Luigi – (standing), Giovanni, Gaspare – (standing), Giuseppe, (circa 1907)[i]

i Not pictured is Florentina, born October 1908.

Author's Note

Giovanni's Last Shoe is the story of Giovanni and Rosaria di Bartolomeo's immigration to America. The book's narrative provides the reader with historical family data and highlights significant events between 1690 and 1945 that were a part of Giovanni, Rosaria, and their children's lives in Torre de' Passeri, Italy, Jersey City, New Jersey, and Baltimore, Maryland. The book does not cover all individuals or generations of the di Bartolomeo family.

The purpose of this book is to provide readers with a consolidated view of the genealogy of the di Bartolomeo family.

It comprises a historical narrative derived from 27 years of genealogical research to provide insight into why the family emigrated, how they lived, and their decision to assimilate into local communities in the United States. Details on location, religion, historical events, education, employment, transportation, politics, and foods of the relevant regions are included in the book to provide context for the events that influenced families' lives at that time.

Giovanni's Last Shoe is a work of non-fiction. The book contains both endnotes and footnotes. Footnotes are identified with Roman numerals and are located at the bottom of the page to provide additional information about specific terms or to clarify information. Endnotes are located at the back of the book and are used to direct the reader to the official source documents and citations for essential facts and details referenced in the book. The citations for dates and events are available in the endnotes.

Some names and dates may be contradictory or have variations in spelling due to family members who changed their first names, surnames, spelling errors, errors in church records, school records, and archives from local government agencies.

Historical data is from Pescara, Italy's Civil Registrations and State Record archives. Marriage records are from Torre de' Passeri town records and microfilm on file in the U.S., Pescara, and Abruzzo, Italy. Weather conditions mentioned in the book either represent the areas' typical weather conditions or were gleaned from historical records, newspaper archives, and actual live weather events.

The residential addresses in the United States for Giovanni, Rosaria, and their children are from United States Federal Census data, cross-referenced with business and residential addresses from WWI and WWII military draft registrations, city directories, employment records, church records, and United States naturalization applications. The stated location of residence will only be accurate as of the exact date of the census survey. Descriptions of transportation used in the book are the typical modes of transportation at that location and the most likely routes available for travel at that time.

Over the past 200 years, schools, businesses, and other institutions have relocated from their original locations. Any building sites referenced in the book will match the facility's location during the historical period referenced in the book. Many buildings, government facilities, and schools have gone through several name changes during the past century. Historically appropriate names are used in the book to coincide with the historical period of the narrative.

The chapter "Giovanni and Rosaria's Children Start Their Own Families" provides details about Maria, Casper, Louis, Anna, George, Albert, and Florence's lives as adults. The children are listed in the order that they left their parents' residence and started their own families. The section "Anti-Immigration and Anti-Catholic Sentiment in the United States" is inserted before the personal details on Casper Lawrence. Although the exact reasons why Casper changed his identity are unknown, during that same time, anti-immigration and anti-Catholic sentiment was increasing.

Chronology of Giovanni and Rosaria di Bartolomeo family residences

YEAR	MONTH	CITY	ADDRESS	RESIDENTS
1855	Jun	Torre de Passeri, Italy	via San Vittorino	Giovanni, Rosaria, Maria, Gaspare, Luigi
1883	Aug	Brooklyn, New York	509 Baltic St.	Giovanni
1895	Jun	Jersey City, New Jersey	157 1/2 Jackson Ave.	Giovanni, Rosaria, Maria, Gaspare, Luigi, Anna, George, Albert
1904	Jun	Jersey City, New Jersey	54 Harrison Ave.	Giovanni, Rosaria, Maria, Gaspare, Luigi, Anna, George, Albert
1906	Jan	Baltimore, Maryland	1301 Eastern Ave.**	Giovanni, Rosaria, Maria, Gaspare, Luigi, Anna, George, Albert
1910	Apr	Baltimore, Maryland	107 W. McComas St.	Giovanni, Rosaria, Maria, Gaspare, Luigi, Anna, George, Albert, Florence, Archie*
1916	Jan	Baltimore, Maryland	Fort Ave. & Light St.[ii]	Giovanni, Rosaria, Gaspare, Anna, George, Albert, Florence, Archie

ii Fort Avenue residence and South Charles Street residence most likely were the same residence, since 1501 South Charles Street is located at the corner of Fort Avenue and Charles Street. The property transfer recorded in 1916 only lists the Fort Avenue property as near Light Street, and the 1920 Federal Census lists the full address of the family as 1501 South Charles Street.

* Argentino Amadio (Archie) was a shoemaker's apprentice that lived with the di Bartolomeo family from circa 1907 to 1920. He emigrated from Montaldo delle Marche, Italy, in 1906 and remained with his family at 1501 South Charles Street after Giovanni moved to Fenwick Ave.

** Address listed on Giovanni's Declaration of Intent. Eastern Avenue may have been a commercial address only and not a residence; the first residence shown in the Maryland Federal Census is W. McComas Street.

1920	Jan	Baltimore, Maryland	1501 S. Charles St.	Giovanni, Rosaria, Gaspare, George, Albert, Florence, Archie
1926	Dec	Baltimore, Maryland	2753 Fenwick Ave.	Giovanni, Rosaria, George, Albert, Florence
1928	Jun	Baltimore, Maryland	2753 Fenwick Ave.	Giovanni, Rosaria, Florence
1931	Apr	Baltimore, Maryland	2753 Fenwick Ave.	Giovanni, Rosaria
1937	Feb	Baltimore, Maryland	2753 Fenwick Ave.	Rosaria

—— CHAPTER ONE ——

1696 - 1892

Italy – Torre de' Passeri, Pescara, Abruzzo
The di Bartolomeo and di Lorenzo Families

The ancient walled village of Torre de' Passeri, defined by its tower, is perched in the mountainous region of central Italy, and everything in it is affected by the dry breezes, short summers, and soft sunlight. The lower valley, Val Pescara, is cut by the Pescara River, providing a consistent flow of fresh, clean water. It is the ideal environment for both noble grapes and resilient people.

The main root of the Montepulciano grape vine creates a network of feeder roots that spread deep into fertile limestone and ferrous clay soil on the outskirts of Torre de' Passeri, seeking the best water and minerals to grow the perfect fruit.

Over the course of 300 years, generations of attentive Abruzzo farmers have perfected the art of growing grapes for Montepulciano d'Abruzzo wine on the lower hillsides. Too much water, and the grapes would be bitter. Too much sun, and the skin of the grapes would burn and wither. The feet of the rootstock, gnarled from decades of standing up to the sun, wind, and occasional predators, defines the dual nature of life, continue to grow and adapt to find joy or wither in the face of adversity.

Giovanni di Bartolomeo stood just as rooted in the ancient volcanic soils of Torre de' Passeri. He was a solid man with a large mustache that ended in two sharp points, hands swollen from years of shaping raw leather into boots, and broad shoulders from his youth working in the fields at harvest. His great-grandfather Giosafatto di Bartolomeo settled in the region in 1739 and built a family life defined by self-reliance and growing what was needed to support his family.

The region of Abruzzo, Italy, bordered by the Adriatic Sea to the east and the Apennine Mountains to the north, has been the home of the di Bartolomeo family dating back to 1696,[1] beginning with Ferdinando di Bartolomeo.[2] Available marriage and birth records indicate that the di Bartolomeo family resided almost exclusively in the small village of Torre de' Passeri, located 70 miles east of Rome and 25 miles west of Pescara and the Adriatic coast. The rugged hilltop village of Torre de' Passeri, where the di Bartolomeo family resided, benefits from the surrounding fertile farmland that produces grapes for winemaking, durum wheat, fava beans, red garlic, and anise. In 1861, the first year of Italy's reunification, Torre de' Passeri had 2,000 residents primarily engaged in agriculture.

Settlement activity in Torre de' Passeri, Pescara, and the Abruzzo region of Italy dates back to 871 A.D., with one of the oldest known medieval castles in the world, the Benedictine Abbey of San Clemente. The abbey was founded in 871 by Louis II,[3] the King of Aquitaine and the great-grandson of Charlemagne.[iii] The ancient church at the abbey contains the remains of Saint Clement, the fourth pope of the Catholic Church, an Apostolic Father, and one of the early popes after the Catholic Church's first pope, Saint Peter. The Benedictine Abbey of San Clemente launched the surrounding areas' initial urbanization and the establishment of a stable population in the region.

Since the collapse of the Roman Empire in 476 A.D., Italians lived under the local rule of feudal regions controlled mainly by the Holy Roman Empire.[4] By the end of the 1700s, the Papal States' control began to diminish while continuously under attack by France, Austria, Prussia, and Spain. By the end of the 1700s, only ten years after the first documented member of the di Bartolomeo family resided in this area, French military leader and emperor Napoleon Bonaparte had conquered Northern Italy for France and declared himself the King of Italy. At the end of the Napoleonic rule, the central regions of Abruzzo and southern Italy were part of the Kingdom of Sicily under the authority of Ferdinand II until 1816. Giovanni's father, Giosaffatte, was born during this period in 1821.

iii Defender of Christianity and emperor of Western Europe from 768–814.

Torre de Passeri, Italy in Val Pescara Region

The walled hill town of Torre de' Passeri in Val Pescara, located in the Abruzzo Region, rises at an elevation of 700 feet and defines the rugged and mountainous surroundings. The village residents built their homes attached to each other, the exterior-facing wall made of stone with few windows, creating fortified, walled houses that enclosed the town in a defensive barrier.

In 1820, a series of revolts encouraged by the Italian Carbonari[iv] began in Turin and Milan, launching a revolution led by the northern Italian Piedmont armies that ultimately led to a united Italy in 1861. The unification of Italy launched a period of rapid growth, primarily benefiting the regions of the north where the new Italian government was developing the Italian industrial base. Torre de' Passeri had bad roads

iv A secret society advancing liberal and patriotic ideas in Italy who opposed Napoleonic rule and the European Bourbon rulers.

and no railroad, making it difficult to reach. Its rural peasant population offered little value to the newly formed government's plan for the industrialization of northern Italy.[v] The Italian government ignored the central and southern regions, believing the area did not advance Italy's industrialization. The reconstruction of the north began a period of neglect in Italy's central and southern providences. This period of neglect profoundly impacted the di Bartolomeo family and led to Giovanni's decision to emigrate from Italy to the United States. The government's lack of investment in reconstruction led to increasing poverty rates and high taxation on the south by northern Italy. This resulted in a suppressed population and economic growth rates of less than 3% per year vs. more than 23% per year for Northern Italy.[5] Additionally, southern Italy did not adopt modern agricultural methods. It was unable to compete with cheap imports from the U.S., so grain production and the agricultural base in southern Italy collapsed.[6]

Giovanni had intimate knowledge of the rampart surrounding Torre de' Passeri. When gathering with his friends on Saturdays, they would march along the four-story-high footpath that connected the towers and adjoining rooftops. From the wall's highest point looking to the northeast, less than 10 miles away, he could view the Abbey of San Bartolomeo, built in 962. As a child, he had scouted every crumbled block, crevice, and fissure in the ancient wall.

---

v During this period, Piombino and Elba (steel mills) were built, and Giovanni Agnelli founded the Fiat Works in Turin.

Giovanni's ancestors were born inside these walls, attended school, married, and raised families inside the 1,000-year-old chiseled stone-block barrier. Over and over, Giovanni considered the current purpose of the enclosed village. Initially, the intent was to protect the town from what was outside of the walls. But Giovanni believed that the walls had become a symbol of confinement, creating an impediment to opportunity. He considered the possibility that the perils of staying inside those walls and not exploring beyond the ancient battlement was more significant than the dangers of what the barriers were keeping out.

Generations of di Bartolomeos in the Abruzzo region were farmers, spinners, weavers, and to a lesser extent, skilled tradesmen such as shoemakers.[7] All marriage records show births and marriages at the same parish in Torre de' Passeri; Chiesa Della Beata Vergine Maria delle Grazie (a.k.a. the Church of St. Mary of Grace) located 300 yards from via San Vittorino, the street where Giovanni was born. Ancestors who married into the di Bartolomeo family from outside Torre de' Passeri came from the nearby villages of Bolognano in the Sant' Antonio Abbate parish, Moscufu, and Chieti. There are no other records for ancestors beyond these regions or earlier than 1696.

Giovanni Antonio di Bartolomeo was born in Torre de' Passeri on June 24, 1858.[8] At 30, he married Rosaria Theresa di Lorenzo, a 20-year-old farmer, on September 15, 1888.[9] Rosaria's father was a shoemaker in Torre de' Passeri.[10] Considering the small size of the village and the fact that both Rosaria's father and future husband were shoemakers, it is likely that Rosaria's father may have employed Giovanni as his apprentice.

Historical records show that Rosaria's father (Angelo di Lorenzo) died on Giovanni and Rosaria's wedding day. Rosaria's three brothers had already decided to immigrate to America, and the loss of Rosaria's father left her mother, Filomena, in a difficult position. The brothers deferred their journey to America until the family had met to consider Filomena's uncertain next phase in life. Filomena's future would take a fortuitous turn, providing her with adventurous prospects that would change her life.

Rosaria di Lorenzo's parents were Angelo di Lorenzo, born November 6, 1837, and Filomena di Nicolantonio, born October 31, 1845.[11] Angelo was the son of Raffaele di Lorenzo, born 1806, and married to Dionora di Nicolantonio, born 1802.[12] Raffaele was the son of Gustino di Lorenzo, born 1774, and Lucia Nicoli, born 1774.[13]

Giovanni's parents were Giosaffatte Antonio di Bartolomeo, a farmer born February 11, 1821, and Annantonio Santoro, a spinner born December 22, 1822. They married on August 5, 1841.[14]

Giosaffatte was the son of Paolo di Bartolomeo, born in 1778, and Nicola Proserzio.[15]

Paolo was the son of Giosafatto di Bartolomeo, born in 1739, and Anna di Tullio, born 1757.[16]

Mandatory military service for all men in Italy allowed the Italian Army to increase education levels for men above the mandatory third-grade level that they received in their rural villages. While Giovanni was in the Italian Calvary, his time away from the village influenced him to consider a future for his family outside the mountain village that had been his ancestors' home for more than 300 years. Generations had improved their welfare in Torre de' Passeri, and Giovanni's children, Maria and Gaspare, were all thriving with the help of his wife, Rosaria.

There were better opportunities for his family outside of the Pescara valley. Recently he had heard from other men in the village and from the public reading of mail in the square that new factories were growing the economy in America and steamships were now providing reliable passage to New York from the Port of Naples.

The decision to depart Torre de' Passeri was more than a determination of risk; it was about changing the family's culture, leaving their church, creating a new future, and leaving behind the history and progress of four generations of di Bartolomeos in the Pescara valley. His ancestors had consistently improved their lives over many years despite historic challenges ranging from the Spanish invasion, smallpox epidemics, Napoleonic rule, and Italy's turbulent reunification. Giovanni's father, Giosaffatte, his grandfather, Paolo, and great-grandfather, Giosafatto, had all managed to improve on the previous generations' welfare.

Giovanni needed to depart Italy and leave the family behind for several years to make his family's immigration to America a reality. If he decided not to make the journey, his children would have limited opportunities for the future, and their experiences in life would be no better than his current situation. If they did not depart while his son and daughter were still young, he was confident that the children would decide to make the journey independently as they grew older and became weary of life in Italy. Leaving while his family was still young would keep the family together. His wife, Rosaria, provided a safe environment for the family while Giovanni traveled ahead to make arrangements for the family to join him in America. Rosaria faced leaving behind her family history in Torre de' Passeri and the Pescara valley, including the center of their social life, the family's church, Santa Maria delle Grazie, and her mother, Filomena. Caring for the children and adapting while a husband immigrated in advance of the family was the life of Italian women in rural Italy in the late 19th century.

Giovanni's steady hand guiding the family and Rosaria's consistent caring for Maria and Gaspare had advanced their lives with everything necessary and improved their standard of living. Deciding to start a 5,000-mile journey across the Atlantic Ocean alone and live apart from his family was a decision that would not be made in haste. *Il buongiorno si vede dal mattino.*[vi]

vi Making a good start ensures a good outcome.

— CHAPTER TWO —

Giovanni's Decision to Emigrate to the United States Emigration to America and The Path to Citizenship

Deciding to emigrate from Italy to America was a difficult decision and one that Giovanni would not have made five years prior. Giovanni based his decision on three issues. Economically, the conditions in Italy's central and southern regions were in rapid decline compared to the extraordinary growth opportunities in America. Reliable transportation, he knew that transportation to the Port of Naples and steam sailor service to America had greatly improved, ensuring safe passage. And he wanted to keep his family together. If he did not make the trip now, he faced the possibility of having his children depart for America on their own one day.

Increasing the uncertainty of the decision was the impact of changing immigration regulations.

Between 1845 and 1850, the flood of immigrants coming to the U.S., primarily from Ireland and England, had tripled over the previous five years. During that time, immigrants were leaving behind difficult living conditions and a future of starvation. Famine in Europe and America's increasing demand for unskilled labor to construct railroads, build canals, and work in factories were all driving immigrants to the U.S. In 1847, 53,000 Irish immigrants took up residence in New York City, which had a population of only 400,000. By the end of the Irish potato famine in 1852, 650,000 Irish had immigrated to the U.S., 75% to New York City.[17] Germans were also fleeing declining economic conditions and high unemployment rates in Germany. The promise of fertile and cheap farmland in the Midwest was the primary factor pulling Germans to the U.S.

The overwhelming demand for unskilled labor, combined with the desperation of people willing to take any risk to flee their lives in Europe, began a period of profiteering from the less fortunate and most vulnerable in the population. Merchant cargo ships that previously carried only commodities were quickly modified to transport humans as below-deck cargo. The transatlantic voyages across the North Atlantic, propelled only by sail, took three to four months. Immigrants made the voyage as passengers living alongside the unusable portion of the ship's steering mechanisms for the three-to-four-month journey. Giovanni considered this a risk, not only to his health but also to his family's overall safety traveling without him. Who would be aboard the ship when his family came to America, and what were the health conditions that could potentially harm his wife and children?

The health and living conditions aboard were miserable for the passengers. Still, many immigrants believed that their chances of surviving the voyage were better than their chances if they were to stay in their hometowns. Sleeping quarters were cramped during the voyage, sleeping two people per bunk with wooden plank beds stacked in threes. The only ventilation below the deck was the open deck hatches if weather permitted. Life-ending outbreaks of smallpox, typhoid, and cholera were common aboard the ships. Passengers trying to improve their chances of a safe voyage brought personal food and utensils but used a communal washtub for cleaning their food and dinner plates, further increasing disease and death aboard the ships.

The risk of death for Giovanni, Rosaria, Maria, Gaspare, and Luigi during their voyage was significant. By 1840, the average mortality rate on ships transporting immigrants across the Atlantic Ocean to the U.S. was 10%. Two ships lost 50% of their passengers while crossing to the U.S. from Europe, and during one year in 1847, 5,000 passengers died aboard ships carrying immigrants to the U.S.[18]

The limited attempts at government regulation to improve conditions aboard the ships failed, since enforcement was under the direction of the ships' captains, and fines were relatively minor.

By the mid-1880s, the federal government had taken notice of the uncontrolled and poorly managed immigration processes in place, and Congress was under pressure to take action. In response, the Carriage Passenger Act of 1885 was enacted in the U.S., which targeted immigration reform and imposed severe penalties for non-compliance. The Carriage Passenger Act defined safety regulations and standards for all ships carrying immigrants for entry into the U.S. The objective was to improve overall conditions for those onboard and establish a consistent immigration framework for entry into the United States. The first initiative was establishing passenger ship density limits at one person per 18 feet of below-deck space, cargo lockers for baggage, 12" ventilators for below-deck ventilation, one bathroom per 100 passengers, separate cooking areas onboard the ship, a doctor and hospital onboard, and chlorine and lime deck-sanitation scrubbing on all deck and gangway areas. To better understand immigration demographics in the United States, the Act also mandated that each ship maintain and provide a written passenger manifest stating the age, sex, occupation, country of origin, and final destination.[19] By 1892, the federal government also oversaw all immigrant entry to the U.S., which was previously under the direction of individual states.

Other forces improved onboard conditions for the di Bartolomeo family when they made their journey. Steamship service almost wholly replaced ships previously under sail power only, reducing the voyage from Northern Europe to New York from approximately 60 days to 14 days, and Italy to New York from almost three months to 18 days. The reduced travel time from Europe to America gave the steamship companies the ability to increase their number of crossings, improve their profits, and set stable transit fares of about $30 per passenger, equal to one month's wages for unskilled labor.[20]

The new regulations did not solve immigration problems in the short term. It took several years for the steamship companies to adapt to the regulations and for new ships to enter the business of transporting immigrants to meet regulations and improve the profits of steamship operators. With the introduction of new ships, improved class of service, and reduced fares, Giovanni was more selective on how, when, and with which shipping companies they planned to make their voyage. In 1892, the Steamship Cachemire, a former cargo carrier on which Giovanni booked future passage, had recently transitioned from transporting coffee from Rio to transporting as many as 700 passengers in a single voyage.[21] One year later, when Giovanni made the voyage in 1893, it only carried 208 passengers. Transatlantic travel conditions were improving; however, even if the family survived the journey, uncertainty existed about when and how—or even if—they would become permanent residents of the United States.

Path to U.S. Citizenship

"To be an American is, unquestionably, to be the noblest, grandest, the proudest mammal that ever hoofed the verdure of God's green footstool. The thought that I am one awakens me with a blast of trumpets."

—— **H. L. Mencken**

Through congressional legislation, the procedures to attain U.S. citizenship changed and evolved every two to five years. Arriving at Ellis Island and other immigration ports of entry in the United States did not provide for nor guarantee that as newly arrived immigrants, the di Bartolomeos were certain to acquire United States citizenship. This uncertainty created more risk, as Giovanni and the family would have no control over the specific immigration legislation in place once they arrived. The change in laws reflected the particular needs of the U.S. at that time, primarily the needs of business and industry, which were dependent on immigrant labor.

In the early and mid-1800s, most immigrants entering the U.S. started businesses and became permanent residents. The profile and motivation of the immigrants coming to America changed after 1860, when most immigrants fled Europe to escape hardships and fill positions as laborers needed to build railroads, canals, and staff factories. Due to the high demand for immigrant labor, many came only to work and earn money in these new jobs before returning home. This second wave of immigrants that came to the U.S. after 1880 included 30–50% of individuals that returned to their home countries after five years. The occurrence of returning workers became so common that the Italians developed a name for them, "Ritornati."

To begin establishing baseline policies on immigration and potential citizenship, the U.S. started initial efforts to formalize and regulate the immigration process, creating immigration laws that defined the path to becoming a U.S. citizen.

<u>On March 26, 1790:</u> The United States Congress passed the First Naturalization Act stating that all free, white adults and their children who had resided in the United States for two years and could prove good moral character were eligible for citizenship.

<u>On April 14, 1802:</u> The United States Congress required the recording of the immigrant's port of entry, name, date of birth, age, country of emigration, and place of intended settlement in the United States.

<u>In 1855:</u> Congress altered the Act to provide spouses with automatic citizenship when their husbands became citizens.

The di Bartolomeo family was subject to the immigration legislation that came into effect after 1900. For Giovanni, Rosaria, Maria, Gaspare, and Luigi to become United States citizens, they were required to denounce their current citizenship and then wait for five years before they could petition the courts and demonstrate their ability to speak

English. The overwhelming challenge for them was that they were only classified as "aliens" during this entire period and designated as temporary residents with no right to vote.

On June 27, 1906: The Act required that if members of the Bartolomeo family applied for citizenship, they would need to demonstrate their ability to speak English.

On May 9, 1918: Congress stated that any foreign-born resident of the U.S. who served three years in the United States military was permitted to file for citizenship without proving the five years of residency. New regulations allowed anyone who served in WWI an exemption from the requirement to file a Declaration of Intent. Foreign-born nationals who served in the U.S. military could now apply for citizenship immediately. Foreign-born nationals represented 18% of the United States armed forces in WWI. More than 300,000 immigrant soldiers who served the U.S. in WWI became U.S. citizens. Gaspare was the only member of the Bartolomeo family who served in WWI, and he did not apply for citizenship.

On September 22, 1922: Married women needed to meet the requirement for naturalization. The Act reduced the residency period from five to one year and waived the requirement for married women to file a Declaration of Intent. If Giovanni became a United States citizen, Rosaria would only be required to demonstrate her ability to speak English.

The U.S. government created immigration and naturalization documents to organize details about the immigrants entering the U.S., including:

1- Certificate of Arrival: When Giovanni arrived in the United States, immigration officials provided him with a certificate stating important information regarding his immigration, including the port of entry, date, age, and passenger list. All members of the di Bartolomeo family arriving from Italy received a Certificate of Arrival when they were processed at Ellis Island. Proper arrival papers were important for Giovanni, Maria, Gaspare, and Luigi, as they were all planning to seek employment and would be required to provide the certificates to their employers when they found new jobs.

2- Declarations of Intent: Giovanni was required to declare his intent to become a citizen and renounce allegiance to the King of Italy, also stating that he was in good standing in his community, not an anarchist, polygamist, nor a believer in polygamy. Giovanni, Maria, and Luigi filed Declarations of Intent every seven years. Giovanni filed his declaration three times while in the United States.

3- Naturalization Depositions: Giovanni needed to provide statements from his character witnesses relating to his good standing as a prospective citizen. Maria and Luigi both had Naturalization Depositions.

4- Naturalization Papers: Giovanni needed to file documents with the courts stating that he met all citizenship requirements. Available records only show that Maria and Luigi filed naturalization papers.
5- Record of Naturalization and Oaths of Allegiance: Certificate of Naturalization granting U.S. citizenship. Available records show that only Maria and Luigi received U.S. citizenship.

In 1893 when Giovanni emigrated to America, 72,000 Italians were immigrating that same year. If the di Bartolomeo family's journey to the United States was a success, Giovanni, Rosaria, Maria, Gaspare, and Luigi would need to complete the formal programs and prescribed court filings. Due to the changing regulations and requirements, there was uncertainty regarding whether the family was ever going to navigate the process entirely and become permanent citizens. It was unknown for how long America would remain "open and welcoming" to immigrants. The timing was important, and the best time to start the journey was now.

—— CHAPTER THREE ——

1893

Beginning the Journey
Torre de' Passeri to The Port of Naples

"Nothing is hard to a man whose will is set on it."

—— **St. Ignatius of Loyola**

The di Bartolomeo family church, Santa Maria delle Grazie in Torre de' Passeri, was designed and built in the classic Catholic Church cruciform design with two intersecting halls forming a Latin cross. A center aisle leading from the back of the church to the front altar is intersected by a transept two thirds up the center aisle, creating a cross with two naves on either end.[22] Located inside the nave on the left is the baptismal font, and the nave on the right houses a cushioned hassock alongside a small altar used for prayer and lighting votive candles for saints and deceased

Family church in Torre de' Passeri, Santa Maria delle Grazie

relatives. Parishioners kneeling in prayer at this altar are comforted by the statue of the Crowned Madonna holding the Christ Child. Constructed from stone and Roman travertine mined at Bagni di Tivoli,[vii] the church has a terrazzo front facade. The front-facing facade of the church has two towers, one on each side. Facing the church, the tower on the left contains a sizeable hanging bell, and atop the tower on the right is a large clock with Roman numerals.

On Sunday, July 23, 1893, the di Bartolomeo family attended Mass at Santa Maria delle Grazie. All members of the parish were present with their families on this particular occasion when the priest delivered a blessing for the safe travels of Giovanni and five other members of the village, departing the next day to begin their intimidating journey to America.

On Monday, July 24, Giovanni, age 35, made the short three-minute walk northwest up via San Vittorino to the Piazza Plebiscito in front of the church. There he met with the other men from the village who were to be his travel companions for the next four weeks.[viii] It was a sunny, pleasant 76-degree July day; light winds were blowing across the wheat fields carrying a barely noticeable scent of anise. During the early morning, the town was quiet, having not yet awakened with the sounds of carts traveling along the cobbled streets and shopkeepers opening their

---

vii Travertine mine located between Torre de' Passeri and Rome.

viii Departure date from Torre de' Passeri was calculated working backwards from Giovanni's arrival date into Ellis Island; August 21 1893, using the number of days to travel to Naples and the recorded voyage dates of his ship.

storefronts. A thin layer of mist burnished the cobbled road of via San Vittorino, creating a slick reflection from the rising sun, highlighting the high spots of the individual stones whose corners were worn down from centuries of use. Giovanni, dressed in dark brown, knee-high leather boots, carried his box of shoemaker tools and a suitcase containing personal items.

The other men of the village ranged from 30 to 56 in age. All from families that had resided in Torre de' Passeri for generations, they had decided to leave the comforting familiarity of the community for America. They were Carmine Cirone, 38 years old, Constantino Petrongolo, a 30-year-old tailor, Angelo Alberici, a 56-year-old stone cutter, Giuseppe Forna, a 32-year-old laborer, and Francesco Favicoli, a 30-year-old carpenter.[23]

Giovanni and the others had spent several months discussing and planning their journey and agreed that now was the right time for their voyage. The decision to leave for America required careful planning to ensure that the trip was successfully completed. In their absence, their families required care, and travel logistics needed to be meticulously reviewed to ensure a good start and that they completed the trip to the Port of Naples, where they intended to board their ship for New York.

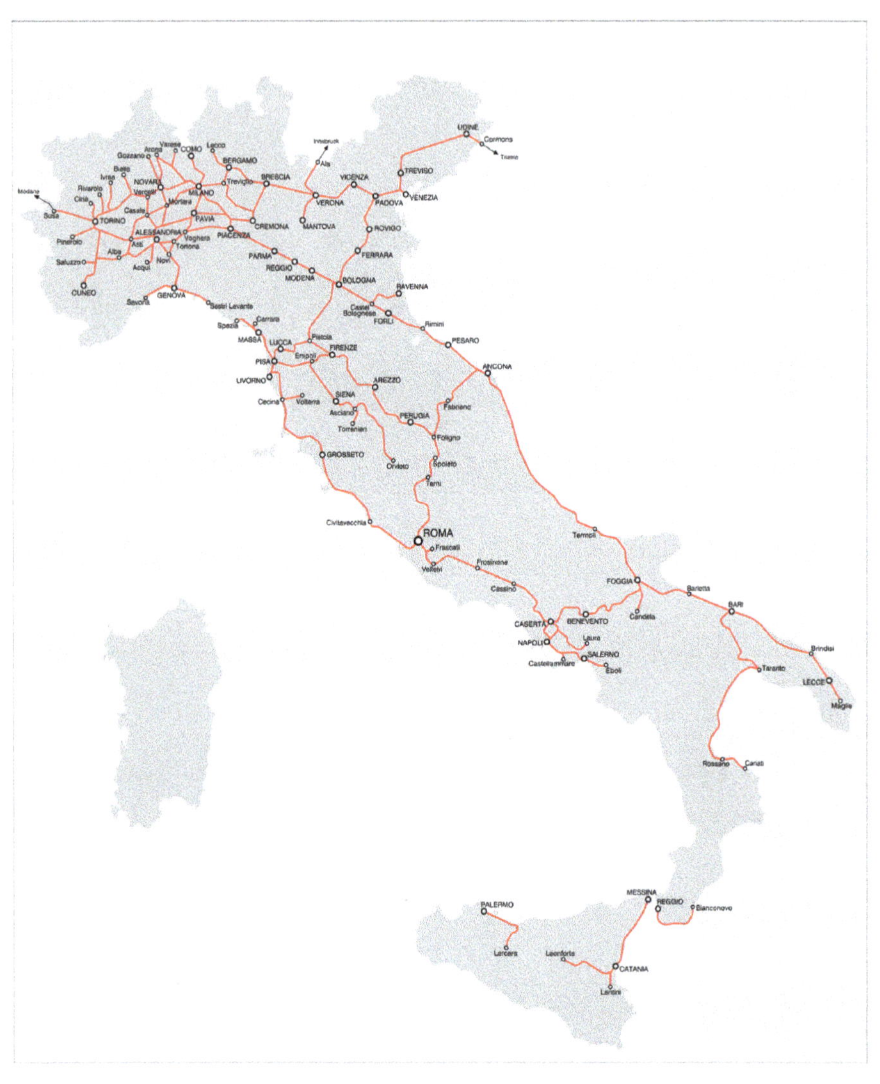

Railroad map of Italy, 1861

Italy had been slow to develop a national train service due to a lack of coal and iron necessary to extend their rail infrastructure. Additionally, as a divided country until 1861, train services remained stubbornly regional. Recently, reliable train service had been made available from the train station in Pescara. With the opening of the Pescara rail station in 1883, one of the early benefits of the unification of Italy was that the Pescara railway was now connected to the Adriatic rail system, allowing for a connection to the Tyrrhenian rail system into the Port of Naples. The rail trip covered 240 miles and took seven hours. They considered the westbound Pescara-Rome railway, connecting in Rome to the Port of Naples. But the rail line between Rome and Naples, was known to be unreliable, having only recently been completed in 1888, and it was subject to landslides along the coast. They were more familiar with Pescara, since it was the center of commerce for their home province. Travel plans were vigorously debated and reviewed, personal affairs settled, and farewells made. They were not returning.

The six men from Torre de' Passeri headed east out of town, taking the provincial road to Chieti. This entailed an 18-mile walk on an unpaved road used primarily by the military and farmers taking sheep to the regional market. The trip to Chieti was an easy five-hour walk, and then they planned to visit relatives in the city and rest for the night.

The next day they departed Chieti at sunrise for a 12-mile walk to Pescara. Giovanni and his travel companions had a leisurely walk along the dirt road to the Pescara train station. The river parallel to the road connecting Chieti and Pescara provided the pleasant sound of rushing water and the occasional view of a red-legged partridge and bean geese. The road was lightly traveled, the serenity only occasionally interrupted by the passing of farmworkers or ranchers pushing their sheep to fields further up the hills. Halfway down the road to Pescara, Giovanni and his travel companions came across a group of eight men traveling from Pescara. Seven men in the group had recently returned from America and were now heading to Chieti. They stopped along the road and exchanged information about their travel plans, soliciting advice for their journey. Four men had taken construction jobs working on bridges, two had worked 12-hour shifts in factories, and one had worked as a tailor in New York. They expressed satisfaction with their time living in America, but their plan had always been to return to Italy. As Ritornati, they were able to amass five years of good salaries to purchase more land in Italy and expand their farms.

The seven men who had recently returned from America were well dressed, wearing wool trousers, tailored waistcoats, billed soft caps, and fine, well-heeled leather boots with substantial buckles and straps. Five years ago, the eighth man did not make the trip to America with his friends, and even though he had planned to travel to America several times, he never made the journey. He was not as well dressed and wore only thin, weather-worn leather ankle boots laced up at the front. His appearance was in contrast with his seven friends. Giovanni was able to tell a lot about a person's journey in life by their shoes.

The men arrived at the Stazione Centrale de' Pescara without incident. They boarded, and the train departed the seaport town of Pescara, heading south along the east coast of Italy, passing small fishing villages and offering the passengers broad views of the blue skies and the Adriatic Sea's green waters. On the west side of the tracks, they passed large groves of recioppella olives, orchards growing vesuvian apricots, and fields filled with San Marzano and Pomodorino tomatoes at the peak of the season. The train maintained a consistent speed of 45 miles per hour, stopping at stations almost every 50 miles as they traveled through Termoli, Foggio, Benevento, and Caserta to reach their final destination, the port city of Naples.[24]

After departing Caserta, the last stop before their final destination, the train approached Naples over a rise, offering an elevated view above the city from the northeast, providing Giovanni with a broad view of the Gulf of Naples and beyond to the Tyrrhenian Sea. The first defining landmark after the flat green water of the Gulf of Naples was the 4,000-foot-high mountain, Mount Vesuvius, the still-active 25,000-year-old volcano located less than three miles from the center of Naples. As Giovanni traveled closer to the city, he noticed that the seaport was framed by an almost perfect 36-mile perimeter horseshoe, providing the port city with a highly protective harbor. The surrounding hillsides of Naples created a tiered amphitheater effect around the city, setting the bustling seaport as the main stage.

Map of Giovanni's Journey to Chieti and Pescara, and Train to Naples

Italian steam engine, circa 1880

As the capital city of Italy's Campania region, located 120 miles south of Rome, Naples's population in 1893 was 536,000. Additionally, the port city hosted hundreds of international travelers and merchants who used the Port of Naples as the primary gateway for their goods to enter Italy. The Napoli Centrale railway station in Naples, completed in 1867, had six tracks and a local rail line running from the city's central area to the seaport, primarily used to carry goods and cargo from merchant ships to the main market areas in Naples. As Giovanni departed Napoli Centrale, he saw the Naples Cathedral, Duomo San Gennaro, the patron saint of Naples and the saint responsible for celebratory Roman Catholic festivals and parades, directly to the east and across the Piazza Nicola Square. The Naples Cathedral, constructed in 1285 and designed in the intersecting formation of the Latin cross with two naves located at each end of the cross, contained the crypt that held the remains of San Gennaro and was also the final resting place of Pope Innocent the IV. The surrounding area of the Duomo was a mixture of two- and three-story granite and marble block buildings mixed with smaller structures that were various shades of red, yellow, and orange travertine.

July 25, 1893, was a typical Tuesday for Neapolitans—vibrant street life mixed with a barely understandable Neapolitan dialect and foreign languages, primarily English and German. To the travelers who recently arrived from Torre de' Passeri, it was unusual to see thousands of people engaged in trading and commerce of every kind. Local citizens on the streets consisted of bakers, butchers, gelato makers, pottery vendors, and fishmongers. Merchants wearing top hats, long coats, and stylish boots accompanied women wearing long dresses and shoes with heels high enough to keep their skirts from hitting the street and head coverings of various shapes and sizes. Children in the streets played games of Volpe e Segugi and Morra.[ix] After a long day traveling from Torre de' Passeri to Naples, the men welcomed a night's rest before meeting the ship.

---

ix Morra is a hand game played by shouting out the sum of the number of fingers shown by the players. Volpe e Segugi is a form of hide-and-seek.

Port of Naples, circa 1900

The next day, they rose at sunrise. The streets were already busy with commerce. Along the central docks, men were knotting their fishing nets while shipyards were busily repairing vessels and setting keels on new ships. Heading toward the port along Via Partenope, the smell of seawater, fresh bread, and coffee saturated the damp air around them. They saw Castel Del Ovo, the ancient castle built on the harbor in the 12th century, and Malo Beverello, the Port of Naples lighthouse, identifying the way to the port as the travelers' primary point of reference to find their ship.

Emigration had become a big business in Naples, not only for the municipal government and local merchants, but also for the Camorra.[x] The port area was overrun with a web of deceptive and insincere sympathetic locals offering to sell unsuspecting travelers everything they

x Criminal society in the region of Campania, Italy.

needed while onboard the ship, from food, drink, and soap to playing cards. Another local business, created to take advantage of peasants, acquired personal belongings like furniture at distressed prices. Once the peasants learned that transporting the furniture they had carted from their homes would cost double and triple the price of their passage onboard the boat, they panicked and sold their family belongings to the local merchants at distressed prices. Even the local Franciscan friars were taking advantage of peasants, offering to sell them prayer cards for comfort during the travelers' arduous journey.[25] Most peasants quickly realized that they were safer onboard the ship than in the Neapolitan crowds.

Walking the remaining three blocks to the area that harbored the departing steamships to America, the travelers noticed half a dozen imposing sailing and steamships in the harbor. Some carried the French tricolor flag, but most carried the Bundesflagge of the Bremen shipping and passenger line. Hearing the voices of people speaking both Italian and English, they worked their way closer. The boarding process was straightforward. They advanced in a line through the immigration station. Then they were required to answer a list of 29 questions, mostly about their occupations, age, point of origin, and final destination or sojourn.

They saw the ship they were to be departing on, the Steamship Cachemire, flying the French flag. The Cachemire was an impressive sight with its blue steel hull towering about 25 feet above the waterline. The "Steam Sailor" was 344 feet in length[xi] with a width of 41 feet, an

xi For reference, ships making transatlantic crossings in 2022 are 1,200 foot in length.

elevated captain's quarterdeck with a wheel at the rear of the ship, a single smokestack with two sails, and a single steam engine turning a rear-mounted propeller.[26] Constructed in 1884, the cargo carrier, which was now nine years old, had seen service worldwide, most recently transporting coffee from Rio de Janeiro, Brazil, to New York City. The passenger transport from Naples was a single class of service carrying 208 individuals to New York City. The food onboard consisted of coffee, boiled meat, boiled fish, salted pork, potatoes, and a hardtack biscuit made from flour, salt, and water that softened as it absorbed the humid sea air or when submerged in coffee. However, for health reasons and to protect against eating contaminated or spoiled food, many passengers only consumed their own tea and bread for the duration of the voyage.

Steamship Cachemire – Painting by Antonio Nicolo, 1886

There appeared to be some confusion occurring at the boarding area. As Giovanni and his travel companions arrived at the departure inspection point, they were greeted by Dr. Young (a surgeon), the American doctor assigned to Naples representing Immigration Commissioner Senner, located in New York.[27] They were required to be checked for any illness and were then issued their passes to board the ship. However, there had been a recent cholera outbreak in Naples, so the U.S. Immigration Service required that all immigrants who boarded the ship in Naples to remain quarantined in the harbor for five days.

After ascending the gangplank, they boarded the Steamship Cachemire, and deckhands stowed the luggage that Giovanni and his travel companions would not need during the voyage. The ship pushed back from the docks and wobbled from side to side as it floated in the harbor for a tedious five days until health officials were able to release the vessel for passage to America. At the end of the five days, Dr. Young boarded the ship and performed medical examinations of all passengers. There was no evidence of cholera, so the Cachemire was released for passage to America.[28] After the medical personnel departed the ship, Captain Gadias, the commander of the Cachemire, blew the steamer's horn three times, the ship's massive propeller cavitated, 2,500 tons of steel shuddered, and the Cachemire pushed forward out of the harbor towards the Tyrrhenian Sea. The departure lifted the spirits of all 208 passengers heading to America, including five families, 29 female passengers, and seven sons and daughters. They came from every walk of life: bakers, butchers, barbers, fruit sellers, shoemakers, stone cutters, dressmakers, millers, carpenters, masons, tailors, and confectioners. Many of the passengers had plans to continue their travels to other destinations —New York City, New Haven, Philadelphia, Waterbury, Brooklyn, Buffalo, and Rochester—on arrival at Ellis Island. The passenger with the furthest destination beyond Ellis Island was heading to Chicago.[29]

On August 20, 1893, *The New York Times* reported: *"In the case of the Cachemire, Dr. Young gave to Capt. Gadias, the commander of that vessel, a letter complimenting him on the efficient manner in which he had conducted affairs during the Cachemire's five-day detention in Naples."*

—— CHAPTER FOUR ——

August 1893

Steamship From Port of Naples, Italy, to Ellis Island

As the ship sailed through the Port of Naples, passengers braced themselves for a journey that would, during its first stage of travel, cover 1,000 miles, taking more than four days just to steam across the Mediterranean Sea, pass through Gibraltar and out into the open Atlantic Ocean. Once they passed through Gibraltar, they would continue traveling the remaining 3,700 miles across the Atlantic to New York in 16 days.

Leaving the shelter of the harbor and beginning their journey, they passed through the Gulf of Naples, with Sorrento, Positano, and the Isle of Capri on their port side. Further out into the Tyrrhenian Sea, they viewed the rocky cliffs on the island of Sardinia on the starboard side and the mountains of Sicily to port. Sailing along the coast of North Africa, they soon saw Casablanca, Morocco, Spain, and Algeria. As they approached the Alboran Sea, they passed through the straits with Gibraltar on starboard and Tangiers to port, marveling at how the continents and the seas came together.

The Atlantic was an endless pattern of rolling and pitching waves, deep blue water, cloud bursts, and occasional shooting stars. Giovanni did not know that a 115-miles-per-hour tropical storm had developed 900 miles south of their position in the West Indies.[30] The storm, classified as a cyclone, was heading northwest to the U.S. coastline. The commander of the Cachemire, Captain Gadias, was highly competent and aware of the potential weather issue, monitoring the storm closely.

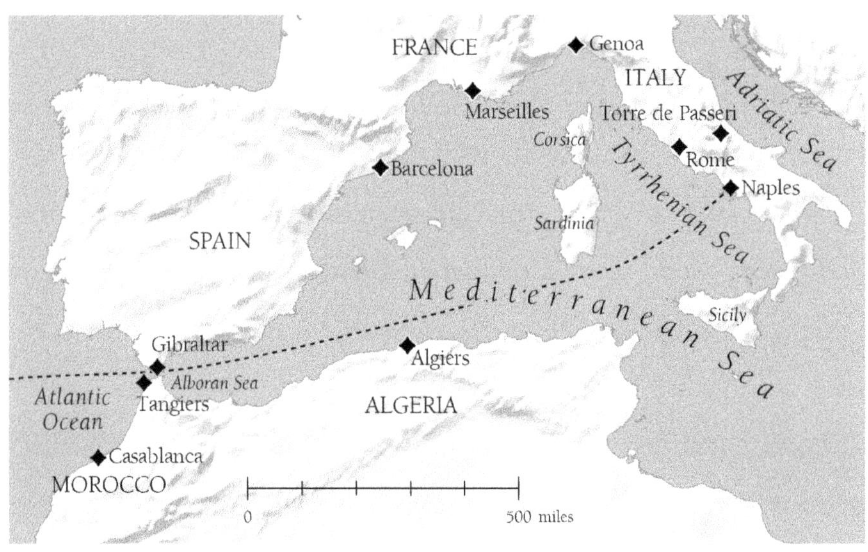

Map of Route Taken by The Steam Sailor Cachemire from Port of Naples to Atlantic Ocean

On the approach to the New York Harbor, the sea was rough, the weather grey, and the skies rainy. The bad weather that started as a tropical storm was now reported as a CAT 3 hurricane. It was presently located in the Carolinas and projected to head up the east coast and make landfall as a CAT 1 hurricane[31] on the coast of New York City and the New Jersey and Long Island regions on August 24th.

Map of New York Harbor and di Bartolomeo Residences While Living in Brooklyn, New York, and Jersey City, New Jersey

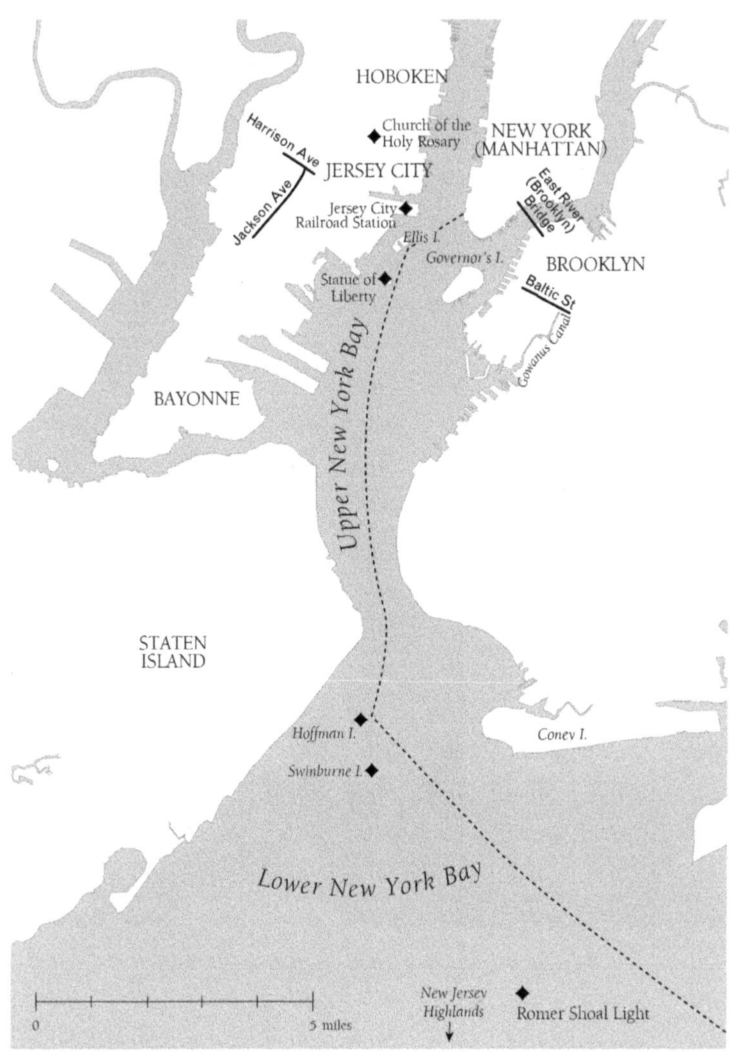

After a 240-mile train journey, five-day quarantine at the Port of Naples, four days sailing through the Mediterranean Sea, and 16 days crossing the Atlantic Ocean, the passengers' journey was almost complete, and everyone's enthusiasm was high. As America came into view, their first sight was the New Jersey Highlands and Romer Shoal lighthouse on the ship's port side. They spotted Coney Island, the East River Bridge, and Governor's Island off the starboard side several minutes later. Finally, straight ahead, they saw the imposing structure and towering torch of the Statue of Liberty, Ellis Island, and the pier where they would soon disembark.

Statue of Liberty -Liberty Island, circa 1900

Hoffman Island, New York Harbor, circa 1900

Once they were within half a mile of Ellis Island, the Cachemire dropped anchor for passenger medical examinations. Immigration Health Officer Jenkins and Dr. Sanborn pulled alongside and boarded the Cachemire from a New York Harbor tugboat. Once the doctors were onboard, they inspected the passengers, looking for illness. Passengers suspected of being sick were transported by ferry to either Hoffman or Swinburne Island, just off the coast of Staten Island.[32] Giovanni and the other 207 passengers would only be able to disembark at Ellis Island if there were no outbreaks of disease or sickness found onboard.

On August 20, 1893, *The New York Times* reported, "*Steamer Cachemire Arrives from Naples with No Cases of Cholera.*"

There were no outbreaks, and the passengers were released to proceed to the ferry boat that transported them to the docks on Ellis Island. There they walked off the ship that had been their home for more than three weeks and onto the island for their first time in America. The processing time at Ellis Island had been streamlined and improved over the years, and the whole process took about seven hours. Food was available for all immigrants on arrival at Ellis. While not the best tasting, it was welcomed by everyone. The meal consisted of bread, prunes, hard-boiled eggs, potatoes, ice cream, and pails of American-style coffee with milk and sugar.[33]

Ellis Island

Once immigration officials directed the weary travelers to proceed forward into the interior of the building, immigration officials used chalk to tag newly arriving passengers with information regarding their personal details and final destination in America. They then moved up the stairs to the registry room for further medical examination and legal review. The doctors efficiently completed a short medical inspection looking for signs of illness by observing whether passengers exhibited any difficulty breathing, walking, or were attempting to hide an illness. If new arrivals were suspected of having any sickness, their jackets were marked with white chalk and they were directed to medical examination rooms. The most rigorous examination was checking the immigrants' eyes, looking for signs of trachoma. If the doctors suspected trachoma, the recently arrived immigrant was pinned with a tag marked with a "CT" and moved to another medical room for a more thorough examination. Trachoma was a bacterial infection, and antibiotics were not available until 1927. Approximately 20% of the arriving passengers were designated with an illness, redirected for quarantine, and eventually cleared for entry. With proper medical attention and early detection of the disease, less than 2% of passengers were sent back to Europe by immigration officials.[34] Most immigrants who never made it into the United States were returned to their home country due to trachoma infections. The immigrants were asked 29 questions to cross-check their personal details listed on the ship's manifest and entry papers. Once they successfully completed their medical review, optimistic immigrants proceeded to the next inspection station for legal inspection. With their processing complete and eager to depart Ellis Island, the hopeful immigrants collected personal luggage. They then exchanged their money, gold or silver, for U.S. currency at the Ellis Island money exchange.

Immigrants exchanging currency and gold for U.S. currency

Bureau of Immigration officials recorded on his arrival that Giovanni was a shoemaker who was able to both read and write, who had resided on the foredeck during his voyage and arrived with two cases, one containing his shoemaker tools and one with personal belongings.[35] Giovanni proceeded forward with fellow passengers and advanced to a staircase divided by two railings that created three separate lanes (stairs of separation) descending into the Great Hall. The left side of the staircase was for passengers departing to Manhattan. The trip to Manhattan entailed a 20-minute ferry ride. The right side of the staircase was for passengers taking the half-mile ferry ride to the Jersey City Central Rail Station for continued travel to other parts of the United States. The center staircase was for newly arrived passengers that required additional medical attention at the hospital. Based on the final destination of the newly arrived passengers, they purchased train or ferry tickets from vendors located in the terminal. They were then directed to the appropriate collection point for transport to that rail or ferry line.

Departing on the ferry from Ellis Island to Lower Manhattan provided Giovanni with an imposing view. The dynamic New York City skyline had 252 buildings that were 10 stories or more, with a variety of domed, spire, jagged, and geometric rooftops. The two most prominent buildings were the 345-foot-tall Manhattan Life Building and the 309-foot-high World Building commissioned by Joseph Pulitzer to house his *World News* publication.[36] Most imposing was the double-arched 272-foot-tall gothic towers of the East River Bridge (Brooklyn Bridge) spanning 1.25 miles over the East River from Manhattan to Brooklyn. Once the ferry from Ellis Island arrived in lower Manhattan, it was only a short walk for Giovanni to the cable car service that took him across the bridge. Once in Brooklyn, the route from the bridge continued for one mile to 509 Baltic Street,[37] located in the heavily industrialized area of Brooklyn at the end of the Gowanus Canal. The Gowanus Canal, constructed in 1849, was an area of Brooklyn concentrated with industrial companies, including coal, gas, chemical, oil, refineries, manufacturers, and most importantly for Giovanni, a tannery[38] and the Hanan Shoe factory employing 1,131 workers in 1893.

Gowanus Canal, Brooklyn, New York, circa 1890

Information documenting Giovanni's time in Brooklyn is limited to a single court record filed on October 18, 1893.[xii] On that date, he was residing at 509 Baltic Street and had filed his Declaration of Intent to become a citizen:[xiii] "*Renouncing forever all allegiance and fidelity to any foreign prince, potentate, state, sovereignty, and particularly to Victor Emmanuel III King of Italy.*" Giovanni's Declaration of Intent was witnessed by Pasquale Parseo, who also lived in Brooklyn.

Three days later, New York City was hit by the hurricane that had threatened them during their voyage. New York and New Jersey experienced 85-mile-per-hour winds, creating a 30-foot storm surge. Two cyclones touched down in New York, inflicting devastating damage.

xii Giovanni refiled his Declaration of Intent again on April 25, 1915.

xiii There are no records documenting that Giovanni received his United States Certificate of Naturalization, only that he met the requirement to refile every seven years.

Brooklyn homes flooded, sewers overflowed, essential services were interrupted for trains and telegraphs, and Central Park was severely damaged, with hundreds of trees uprooted.

On August 25, 1893, *The New York Times* reported: "*New York has seldom suffered more by the elements. The low parts of the city, the districts lying along the waterfronts on both the east and the west side were flooded. The rain washed out gutters and manholes and did much damage to many of the streets. Hundreds of chimneys were tossed down like playthings, and roofs were ripped off as if with a knife.*"

The industrial community in Brooklyn was Giovanni's home in America until he relocated two years later, in 1895, to 157 ½ Jackson Avenue, Jersey City, N.J.[39] Giovanni relocated in preparation for Rosaria, Maria, Gaspare, and Luigi's arrival in America on January 12, 1897.[40] Giovanni's priority was that his wife and three children would arrive to a safe and comfortable home in a community large enough to support his shoemaking business and with a Catholic church. The family's new church was initially St. Patrick Catholic Church[xiv] in Jersey City.[41]

Three and a half years had passed since Giovanni departed Torre de' Passeri. The time away from family was almost over, and family members anticipated the reunion. The anxious family members, Rosaria, Maria, Gaspare, and Luigi, were fortunate to depart Naples on a more modern and faster steamship. Their ship first stopped in Genoa and Gibraltar

---

xiv Anna Bartolomeo, the first child born in the United States, was baptized in 1897 at St. Patrick Church. Afterwards the family changed parishes to the Church of the Holy Rosary, where Giuseppe was baptized.

after leaving Naples for the ship's final destination, Ellis Island. In January 1897, Rosaria and the three children departed from Italy, experiencing cold weather and snowy conditions on their winter voyage across the Atlantic.

After the family arrived and completed their processing at Ellis Island, Giovanni met them on the first floor of Ellis Island's Great Hall, where family members waited to greet newly arrived members of their family. The family reunion in the Great Hall of Ellis Island was the first time that Giovanni met and held his son Luigi, who was born eight months after Giovanni left Italy for America. Luigi, two years old and newly arrived at Ellis Island, was with his father for the first time. Glowing, Giovanni took his family to their new home in Jersey City.

—— CHAPTER FIVE ——

1905/1906

Jersey City and Train to Baltimore

Rosaria and her children traveled from Italy to Ellis Island on the Steamship Werra. The German steamship company recently began operating the Steamship Werra on an exclusive route from Naples to Genoa to Gibraltar to Ellis Island. The steamship was a modern express steamer with a crew of 11 that carried 26 first-class passengers and one small dog; all U.S. citizens, 10-second class, 181 in steerage, including seven infants. It traveled at 18 knots and made the trip from Naples via Genoa and Gibraltar to Ellis Island in 16 days.

The Steamship Werra

On January 12, 1897, Rosaria di Lorenzo (30), born July 15, 1867,[42] her daughter Maria (eight), born December 1, 1889,[43] sons Gaspare (five), born July 7, 1892, and Luigi (two years, 10 months), born March 29, 1894,[44] arrived at Ellis Island on the Steamship Werra.[45] When they arrived in New York Harbor, the January weather was a chilling 23 degrees with snow and hail. The ship's manifest indicated that Rosaria and the children had arrived from Naples via Genoa and were steerage-class passengers in the aft compartment. Rosaria, the daughter of a farmer, wife of a shoemaker, and traveling with three small children, arrived at Ellis Island with one suitcase as the family's sole possession.[46]

During Giovanni's absence from the family, communication was unreliable and limited. It was difficult for the family to share information while Giovanni was in America. Written correspondence between Giovanni and Rosaria took more than three months. Sometimes Giovanni was fortunate to locate a Ritornati and would give them a letter to post in Naples on their arrival in Italy. The letter was then carried from Naples to Pescara by train and posted in Chieti. Otherwise, Giovanni had the opportunity to post the letter directly with a returning steamship whose final port was Naples.

One of the challenges that new immigrants faced was maintaining communications with their family members who remained behind in their countries of origin. Until they were reunited, families relied on private mail services, immigrants returning to Europe, or new arrivals to the U.S. carrying letters to family members. The postal service did not provide consistent international mail services from the United States until 1875,[47] when the international postal congress set procedures for handling mail between the U.S. and Europe. Another alternative, telegraph cable communications, was not in service between the U.S. and Europe until 1866.[48] Additionally, immigrants from rural villages had yet to establish local post offices, and it would be decades until rural villages had any reliable electronic telegraph communications.

Once delivered to the correct destination, low literacy rates impacted the writing and reading of mail between families and required the services of people who were able to read and write. Generally, the task of reading the letters occurred in public squares.[49] This practice undoubtedly influenced immigration in rural villages, where people became encouraged by the news from America. Reading mail in the public squares provided a practical way for immigrants to learn of logistics for travel and advice on ensuring a safe journey.

While in the U.S. Giovanni continued to prosper. He had worked for three and a half years, making shoes to earn enough money for Rosaria and their three children to join him in America. During the past eight years in Jersey City, he had built expertise in negotiating U.S. commerce and the confidence to expand his business.

After arriving in the U.S., the di Bartolomeo family added three more children to their growing household. Anna was the first of the di Bartolomeo children to be born in the U.S. Anna was born on December 2, 1897,[50] Giuseppe on February 23, 1899,[51] and Alberto on October 20,

1900;[52] all in Jersey City. Still to come was Florentina (Florence), who was born on October 5, 1908,[53] once they settled in Baltimore.

Giovanni had decided to relocate the family to Baltimore from New Jersey. Changes to modernize the shoemaking trade were underway, and he found better growth opportunities in Baltimore. By the late 1800s, the bespoke "village-based shoemaking industry" was transitioning to a "cottage industry" business model. The new manufacturing process allowed shoe factories to provide shoe patterns to shoemakers, who selected the animal hides, cut the leather parts to specifications, and sent the individually cut pieces to the central factory location to be sewn together. In the short term, this was an opportunity for Giovanni. In addition to continuing to craft new shoes on a bespoke basis for individual customers who came to his shop, Giovanni was now becoming a supplier for the growing, centralized shoemaking trade. The average cost for a pair of women's shoes at the time was $2.80.[54] Giovanni was ready to expand his business and made arrangements to take on a shoemaker's apprentice, Argentino Amadio who would join the di Bartolomeo family in Baltimore.[55]

On an unusually windy fall day in 1905,[xv] all members of the di Bartolomeo family assembled on the green iron train platform of the Central Railroad of New Jersey Terminal dressed smartly in wool suits

---

xv U.S. Federal Census shows the family residing in Jersey City in 1905. On January 8, 1906, Giovanni signed his Declaration of Intent for Citizenship in the U.S. Circuit Court of Baltimore, so they relocated to Baltimore between June 1905 and January 1906. Address listed is 1301 Eastern Avenue, Baltimore, MD.

and high-top laced boots. The oldest daughter, Maria, wore one large ribbon in her hair, and the youngest daughter, Anna, had two bows arranged atop her head. The older boys were dressed in suits and ties, and the youngest boys were wearing sailor suits. All were under the attentive eye of their sister Maria as they eagerly awaited the B&O southbound railroad car #525 with a mid-afternoon departure to Baltimore.[56]

Looking to the east, all six children would have been able to see Ellis Island, where their father Giovanni had first landed in America from Torre de' Passeri. It was only 12 years ago that their father, at age 35, arrived with plans to begin preparing for the family's new life.

From 1880 to 1910, 20 million Europeans, including four million Italians, fled poverty and famine for the United States. The search for jobs and money seemed to be pulling everyone westward.

Central Railroad of New Jersey Terminal

To the di Bartolomeo family, it appeared that on this day, all four million had converged on the Central Railroad of New Jersey Terminal located in Jersey City. The enormous size, deafening sounds of locomotives, bewildering languages, and rush of people through the terminal platforms were overwhelming. The massive Romanesque red brick structure dominated the west bank of the Hudson River directly across from Manhattan. The terminal clocktower with its large Roman numerals overlooked the Statue of Liberty and Ellis Island to the east. The gable-roofed, multi-modal terminal saw 40,000 people arriving and departing per day. The terminal complex was so large that in addition to the 20 train platforms, the imposing structure also accommodated five ferry terminals that completed 128 daily ferry runs between New York City and Ellis Island. The transportation complex served as a central hub, connecting incoming immigrants with 132 daily train departures through the imposing structure of the Central Railroad of New Jersey Terminal.

The children were apprehensive about relocating from 54 Harrison Avenue in Jersey City[57] to their new home in Baltimore.

Once they arrived in Baltimore, Anna, George, and Albert would enroll in new public schools. In Jersey City, all three children had an easy walk to Elementary School #14 on Union Street, four blocks from the first home on Jackson Avenue, and then PS #12 on Crescent Avenue, two blocks from Harrison Avenue.[xvi]

xvi Both schools advised that they did not keep student records longer than 10 years. Holy Rosary advised they had no school records for the di Bartolomeo children. No records were found during a search of the N.J. Historical Society and Hudson County School Systems.

Church of The Holy Rosary, Jersey City, where the family attended Mass and Giuseppe and Alberto were baptized

They were uncomfortable leaving behind the center of their family life, Chiesa Italiana Del Santissimo Rosario (The Church of the Holy Rosary), several blocks away on 6th Street, where family members attended daily Mass. The Italian-speaking population of Jersey City had increased so rapidly to a congregation of over 10,000 Italian immigrants that in

1895, the existing church building had to be expanded. The Church of the Holy Rosary would become the oldest Italian Roman Catholic Church in New Jersey. For Anna, Giuseppe, and Alberto, this was the only home they had ever known. However, they were well cared for, enjoying their lives, and were looking forward to a new adventure.

The Marylander

The family planned to depart Jersey City on the Baltimore and Ohio railroad locomotive, "The Marylander." Their steam-engine powered train originated across the river from New York Rockefeller Station, with stops at New York Grand Central Terminal and then Jersey City. The ticket to Baltimore was $3.80 per person, approximately two cents per mile. Giovanni, Rosaria, and the six children planned to travel the short 185 miles in less than eight hours with stops in Elizabeth, Plainfield, Philadelphia, Wilmington, and Baltimore's Mt. Royal Station, with Baltimore's Camden station as the final destination. Camden Station was only a short streetcar ride from their new home at 107 West McComas Street,[58] located less than one mile from Fort McHenry, where Francis Scott Key penned "The Star-Spangled Banner."

Their new church, St. Mary, Star of the Sea, was located in South Baltimore. It had a bright maritime beacon on top of its spire that welcomed sailors into the Port of Baltimore. The church was constructed in 1884 to serve the expanding population of sailors, shipbuilders, and workers on the Baltimore and Ohio railroad.

The wind blew westward across the charcoal gray waters of the Hudson River, and the 15-plus-mile-per-hour winds penetrated through the open steel columns of the Jersey City Railroad Station. By mid-afternoon, the terminal had reached its peak activity of the day. All of the family's household possessions, furnishings, three trunks of linens, and clothing had already been loaded on the attached freight car. The scream of the 600-ton train cars on iron rails, the smell of creosote, high-pressure steam releasing from boilers, and the whining of electric locomotives drowned out everything and everyone except for the station conductors calling out cities and platform numbers. *"Now boarding on Track 5; The Marylander with service to Elizabeth, Plainfield, Philadelphia, Wilmington, Baltimore Mt. Royal Station, Baltimore Camden Station, Washington, D.C., and Wheeling West Virginia."* **Buona Fortuna e Buon Viaggio.**[xvii]

---

xvii Good luck and safe travels.

After briefly stopping in Philadelphia,[xviii] "The Marylander" made a scheduled two-hour stop in Wilmington, Delaware. During the stop at Wilmington Station, there was an opportunity for the di Bartolomeo family to visit with Rosaria's mother, Filomena. Filomena had immigrated to the United States on April 7, 1896,[59] from Torre de' Passeri.

At age 52, Rosaria's mother, Filomena Nicolantonio di Lorenzo, had made the journey from Italy to Ellis Island alone. This was only eight years after the death of her husband Angelo, who died on Giovanni and Rosaria's wedding day. Before Filomena arrived in America, Rosaria's three brothers had immigrated to the United States, relocating to Minneapolis, Brooklyn, and Jersey City. The known facts of Filomena's life in the U.S. are limited, except for government records documenting her immigration through Ellis Island on April 7, 1896. U.S. military records also confirm that she had remarried and became the wife of Tony Verrosso, an Italian-United States military veteran. Filomena's second husband, Tony Verrosso, had formerly been a police officer in Rome, Italy,[60] served in the U.S. infantry, and was a veteran of the Spanish American War. Tony held the rank of Private, serving in the Wilmington, Delaware, First Infantry, Company H.M.[61] After the Spanish and American War, Tony and Filomena moved to Washington, D.C. On

---

xviii In a 1984 interview, Anna Bartolomeo states that the train stopped in Washington, D.C., "which was the stop just before Baltimore," and then "continued to the next stop Baltimore" because Giovanni did not like the area around the Washington, D.C. train station. It is likely that she misstated Washington for Wilmington, since Wilmington is the stop prior to Baltimore, and D.C. was the stop after passing through Baltimore and continuing on to Wheeling, West Virginia. Additionally, Rosaria's mother was living in Wilmington at that time.

August 1, 1906, *The Washington Post* reported that *"President Theodore Roosevelt appointed Tony Verrosso to a position at the U.S. Government Printing Office."*[62]

Tony Verrosso may have been a family friend or distant relative from Italy. The Verrosso name appears in the di Bartolomeo family genealogy in the early 1800s. Filomena's mother's maiden name (Rosaria's grandmother) was Verrosso; "Francesca Verrosso." The Verrosso family was located in Castiglione a Casauria, Pescara, Abruzzo, Italy,[63] less than a 45-minute walk from Torre de' Passeri.

The Washington, D.C., residential directories document that Tony and Filomena resided at 15 H Street NE and 3200 10th Street NE, Washington, D.C. in 1922. U.S. Military records show that Tony received a U.S. War pension of $12.[64] Filomena di Lorenzo (now Filomena Verrosso), born October 31, 1845, died September 21, 1930,[65] and Tony Verrosso, born (date unknown), died on December 28, 1928.[66] Filomena and Tony are buried at Arlington National Cemetery, Section W ENL, Site 21348.[xix]

The di Bartolomeo family was now only 70 miles north and less than 90 minutes from their destination in Baltimore. Giovanni was anxious to get to Baltimore to set up his business. Fatigue had set in with the children, and Rosaria was ready to get to their new residence. With the new school year starting in January, family members anticipated, with varying degrees of concern, registering for school, finding new employment, and getting

xix U.S. ref. ID. 330388 Arlington National Cemetery, lot # 21348.

to know the neighbors. On a December day in 1905, the family had completed their journey, and for most of the family members, Baltimore was the final destination, where they spent the rest of their lives.

— CHAPTER SIX —

1906 to 1916
Baltimore, Maryland

The 1910 Federal Census for Baltimore Ward 23 shows that the di Bartolomeo family possessed the only Italian surname in the South Baltimore neighborhood of McComas Street where they were living. There were no other Italian surnames listed in the neighborhood. With many Italian neighborhoods in Baltimore, such as Baltimore's prodigious Little Italy just east of the Inner Harbor available to the family, the di Bartolomeos had chosen to live in an area dominated by Irish and German immigrants. All neighborhood residents were born in Maryland, Virginia, Pennsylvania, and Delaware or had recently immigrated from Germany, Ireland, or England with surnames like Mueller, Hiller, Murphy, and Buckholtz. Their neighbors' occupations also reflected the high growth "new economy" businesses and industries dependent on immigrant labor at the time. As the largest employer in the area, the B&O Railroad employed the men, and the women worked as seamstresses and pressers for the local shirt factory.[67]

Many changes occurred for the family in Baltimore. When the

children started attending school and the older children took on new jobs, the family's assimilation into American culture accelerated. First names were Americanized, positions taken as skilled tradesmen, properties acquired, new businesses started, and other family members continued their migration to other parts of the country in search of opportunities. Along the way, education and the influence of the Roman Catholic Church remained a priority and played a central role in the family's development.

When the family arrived in Baltimore, it was the fourth largest city[68] in the United States.[xx] Baltimore had become a rapidly expanding and important east coast location for culture, finance, and manufacturing. Booming port infrastructure and consistent inflows of immigrant labor was a driving force behind the growth of Baltimore's garment factories, steel mills, and railroad operations. The new center of commerce also created prosperity, and that wealth improved the lives of all residents of Baltimore. Local philanthropists used their new fortunes to improve education, access the arts, and build world-class healthcare facilities. Two notable individuals at the time were Johns Hopkins and Enoch Pratt. Johns Hopkins, the son of a Quaker tobacco planter, moved to Baltimore at 17.[69] He became wealthy from real estate and was an early investor in rail transportation, becoming the largest single shareholder of the B&O Railroad, which in 1827 was the first railroad to provide passenger service. To improve the city, he organized two corporations; one for a hospital

---

xx Baltimore was number four, behind New York City, Philadelphia, and Brooklyn.

and another for a university. The Johns Hopkins Medical Center and Johns Hopkins University went on to lead public health and medical research for Baltimore and globally. Enoch Pratt, who made his fortune in steel, canal, and rail transportation, established the Enoch Pratt – Free Library in Baltimore. Andrew Carnegie saw Enoch Pratt as a pioneer and stated, *"Many free libraries have been established in our country, but none that I know of with such wisdom as the Pratt Library in Baltimore."*[70]

When the di Bartolomeo family arrived in the city in 1906, Baltimore continued its rapid growth and redevelopment after the devastating fire of 1904. The fire, caused by a discarded cigarette in the basement of the Hurst building, had destroyed more than 25 blocks of businesses and homes in Baltimore.[71]

Locust Point with Fort McHenry in the foreground (modern day)

South Baltimore, where the di Bartolomeo family initially resided, was located on the western edge of Locust Point. The city heavily invested in developing South Baltimore's Locust Point area in 1884 to improve access to the growing port system. The demand for more workers also created a high demand for housing. Most of the Locust Point row houses were built between 1884 and 1901, and they tended to be smaller than other row houses built at the time, which were grander, with covered porches and daylight bay windows.[72] The di Bartolomeo townhouse had gas lighting, coal heating, and no indoor toilet.[xxi] The 1910 U.S. census lists the di Bartolomeo family renting the 12-feet-wide, two-room-deep brick house at 107 West McComas Street. The new home in Baltimore on McComas Street was also ideally located only two blocks from a slaughterhouse.[73] A short walk north to East Winder Street[xxii] and Giovanni had convenient access to the animal hides required for his business. Giovanni and his family did not stay at this address for an extended period and moved to Fort Avenue in Baltimore, located three blocks away,[74]sometime between 1916 and 1920. On January 20, 1916, the *Baltimore Sun* newspaper reported a real-estate transfer from Walter J. Gauer to Giovanni di Bartolomeo and his wife for an address at Fort Avenue, Baltimore, near Light Street, for a ground rent of $42.[xxiii]

---

xxi It was not until 1905 that voters backed a plan for a comprehensive system of building separate storm and sanitary sewers, including primary and secondary treatment of human waste. Prior to this, cesspits and privy vaults were common.

xxii Based on Sanborn historic fire insurance maps.

xxiii The family lived at this address until relocating to 1501 South Charles Street.

Baltimore was erecting many new factories on the waterfront, and the recently constructed, largest steel mill in the U.S. was transforming the area, employing 30,000 full-time workers. The steel mills became the center of life for many families in the "company towns" in Sparrows Point, housing more than 9,000 people on the 2,500-acre site. The steel mill baseball teams were central to local amusement and entertainment for steel mill families. The steel mill league fielded six teams with competitive players, including former professional baseball players Babe Ruth, "Shoeless" Joe Jackson, and Roger Hornsby.[75]

Because of the transportation infrastructure connecting Baltimore's seaports with rail terminals, the city became a center for canning operations, leading the country in the canning of oysters, fruit, vegetables, and seafood. The new infrastructure made Baltimore one of the largest industrial centers on the east coast and a significant center for rail operations, with rail lines transporting coal, coke, limestone, and iron for steel mills and distribution of finished products. Four rail lines served the steel mills on Sparrows Point—Western Maryland Railroad, Pennsylvania, B&O, and Patapsco Rail lines. Clothing manufacturers were also expanding in Baltimore, and Maria worked at one of these as a seamstress.[76] Some of the largest in the city were Erlanger Brothers Clothing, makers of the famous BVD undergarments, and Gans Brothers, the largest umbrella maker in the U.S., with the slogan, "Born in Baltimore – Raised Everywhere."

The family members easily integrated into their community, taking advantage of the accelerating economic growth, jobs at newly created businesses, attending schools, and leading an active social life at the church. The family added a baby girl, Florentina (Florence), born in Baltimore on October 5, 1908. Argentino (a.k.a. Archie) Amadio,[xxiv] Giovanni's apprentice, also lived with the family in the Bartolomeo home at 107 West McComas Street.[77]

Giovanni's shoemaking business operated from inside the family home.[78] Customers used the street-level front entrance to visit Giovanni's shoe shop; the second floor was the family living space, and the third floor provided sleeping quarters for the family. The front entry was reserved for business customers, while the family used the side entrance. Giovanni made shoes, repaired shoes, and had three cane-back chairs for when he was shining customers' shoes in the shop. George and Albert worked in the shoe shop on Saturdays, and Giovanni allowed the two brothers to keep what they earned from shining shoes. In addition to the coming and going of customers, the house was full of seven active children, two parents, two workers, and a cat that took up residence on top of the family icebox. The sounds from the shop and house all came together in a symphony of shoemaking and household activities. It was the tap-tap-tap of the shoemaker's last hammer, the pop-pop-pop of the awl and punch driving through the leather to brogue the shoe, and the snip-snip-snip of gimping scissors cutting the leather to create the jagged edge designs. While Anna played the piano and Maria operated the sewing machine,

---

xxiv Argentino (Archie) was a shoemaker's apprentice that lived with the di Bartolomeo family from circa 1907 to 1920. He was born 1888 in Italy, immigrated to the U.S. in 1906, and naturalized as a U.S. citizen in 1918.

Rosaria worked non-stop, cooking, cleaning, and washing laundry for seven children. Six days a week, Giovanni kept the shop open until 8 p.m., and Rosaria would carry meals down to the shop for him and the other workers.

Rosaria's life was challenging but fulfilling; however, it was a time of isolation for her—isolated first in Torre de' Passeri with no husband, and then isolated in America because they lived in neighborhoods with no Italian neighbors, which meant no one spoke Italian.

She was indefatigable as a mother of seven and relentless in her support of Giovanni to improve their children's well-being. Rosaria Bartolomeo did it all quietly and confidently. The burdens that she took on improved the welfare of her children.

Giovanni was a successful shoemaker because he could visualize what his clients wanted in a shoe when they described them. He knew his customers' personalities and used the best materials and designs to exceed their expectations. Becoming a shoemaker required Giovanni to work years as an apprentice to develop the necessary skills working with wood, leather, cork, and lanolin to master the perfect fit, quality, and appearance. These skills were not easily mastered. More importantly, it required a passion for creating a product by hand that Giovanni would be proud to put to his name.

Giovanni required tanned hides to make leather for shoes. The typical tanning process at that time was vegetable tanning. This entails submerging the animal hide in a mixture of water and vegetable oil made from the tannins of oak and chestnut for two to three months to ferment the skins. The final leather product has a sweet, woody smell similar to the plants used in the tanning process.

The ultimate goal, achieving the perfect fit, is challenging because the foot consists of 33 moving joints, 26 bones, and 100 muscles, tendons, and ligaments. Giovanni took many measurements when first beginning to make a shoe, tracing the client's foot in a sitting and standing position. Giovanni would then carve, scrape, and sand the woodblock to the foot's shape. After carving the block, he would have a three-dimensional model and a last to begin making a paper pattern for the individual pieces of leather that needed to be cut and sewn together to make the shoe.

L-R, Shoemakers last, gimping scissors, punch, waxed cord, last plyer & hammer, awl, hammer.

Once Giovanni made paper patterns that became the leather upper, including the location of eyelets and tongue, toe, heel, lower and sole, he then used these patterns to cut the leather into pieces.

Using the paper patterns made for each piece of leather, Giovanni would cut six individual leather pieces for the shoe, known as "clicking" the leather. For shoes that needed to be stylish, similar to wingtips, Giovanni would cut the leather pieces with gimping scissors that created a decorative, jagged edge. To generate the brogue effect, shallow holes in the leather, he would use a punch to make the shallow, decorative holes. To soften the inside of the shoe, he would sew in a lining to the upper portion of the shoe for a comfortable fit. Once he had all the individual leather pieces from the paper pattern, Giovanni would start sewing them together. The edges were skived so that the leather pieces would lie together uniformly when overlapped for stitching.

Giovanni would use thread treated with beeswax and pine resin to sew the pieces together. As the waxed cord was rapidly pulled through the holes, the wax would soften and seal the holes.

Once the pieces were stitched together, he would place the leather sole against the bottom of the wooden last and glue cork filler to the bottom of the inner sole. He would then glue the outer sole over the cork and the inner sole on the bottom of the shoe. Once finished, he would remove all wrinkles from the leather upper and make a heel by stacking and gluing pieces of leather together to achieve the desired height.

In the final step, he would remove the wooden last from the shoe.

Giovanni would now have a shoe ready for finishing with polish, laces, or straps to deliver to his customer.

Giovanni was committed to his work, and he was pleased to see that his efforts had built a successful business, allowing him to provide for his family. At closing, Giovanni spent time with his workers, sampling his homemade wine and playing a boisterous game of Morra, a 3,000-year-old Italian hand game played by guessing and shouting out the sum of the fingers on two opposing players' hands. The traditional game was used to settle disputes between two people, designating the person that shouted out the correct sum to be the winner of any disagreement.

Baltimore was the home of the first electric streetcar, and most of the horse-drawn trolleys had already been converted to electric by the time the family moved there. The road outside the di Bartolomeo house was always busy with streetcars passing the home, sounding their bells, stopping on the corner, allowing people to visit Giovanni's shop, or spending time at the saloon across the street that also had a pool table. The new streetcar line was also the preferred method for the di Bartolomeo children to explore around town or attend a movie at the movie theater. The streetcar line allowed passengers to ride the line from 25th and Howard Street to 40th Street for five cents. On many days the customer traffic in Giovanni's shop were young women ordering new shoes. The groups of young ladies often included several girls from Goucher Women's College entering the shop, chewing gum, and wearing mid-calf hemline skirts with tall button-up boots.[79] Local men would bring their worn boots in for repair. On Saturdays, George and Albert worked in the shop shining shoes, adding the aroma of lanolin and turpentine polish to the air already thick with the smell of fresh-cut leather, glue, and Rosaria's cooking.

The family meal always included maccheroni or chitarra, the traditional pasta of the Abruzzo region. Rosaria would lay the flour on the table and crack three eggs, mixing them to make the pasta. She would then roll out the pasta on the table, cut it into thin flat strips, gently boil it, and serve it with vegetables and a dandelion salad. Fresh fruit for dessert often followed dinner.[80]

The aroma of onions, garlic, and oregano was always present along with the scent of cedar, chestnut, and oak bark—used in the vegetable tanning solution—and wax and oils used to finish the leather. Giuseppe recalled that the family's bathtub was rarely available for baths since it was constantly being used for soaking animal hides. Hence, they could be tanned to Giovanni's requirements and then worked into soft leather for shoes.[81] For centuries Italian shoes were known for their fine craftsmanship using the highest quality leather. There were villages in northern Italy that bred cattle for the sole purpose of yielding the finest hides. The leather-tanning process in Italy was built on multi-generational trade secrets by those with a passion for fine work. The animal hides were soaked in water and oils from vegetables, tree bark, and leaves for up to three months and stretched on wooden drums to smooth the top grain. The tanning process of using vegetables and water created a rich cordovan appearance, supple texture, and proteins that gave Italian leathers their distinct smell. The method of vegetable tanning required 40 days. Once tanned, Giovanni worked the top grain leather with his hands to soften it and make it ready for cutting and stitching. Since chemicals were not used to seal the hides, the leather took on the character and color of its environment.

As the only Italian family in the neighborhood, the di Bartolomeo family never experienced complications or had worries about their neighbors in the community. On occasion, "Mano Nera," the Black Hand, visited Giovanni's business looking for money.[82] The Black Hand were gangsters who extorted money from business owners. The Black Hand in Baltimore was led mainly by recent immigrants from the Calabrian region of Southern Italy.[83] Prior to 1860, Italians coming to Baltimore had money to invest and emigrated mostly from Genoa to start new businesses. In the early 1900s, this changed when Mezzogiorno immigrants from Italy migrated from Naples, Abruzzo, Cefalu, and Palermo. Immigration patterns in the United States had changed, and with the change came a segment of the population that had different motivations for coming to the U.S.

One of the reasons Giovanni may have decided not to live in an Italian neighborhood was to avoid the culture and efforts of Mano Nera, which was minimized by living in an Irish and German community.[xxv] Another reason that Giovanni may have settled in non-Italian neighborhoods was to accelerate the family's assimilation into American culture. Also, knowing that Americans perceived Italian immigrants as inferior, he could separate himself from unjustified generalization about Italians by being the most diligent and studious Italian family on the block.

Italian was spoken in the home and broken English in the shop. The children were fluent in English from attending school and playing with friends. They were doing well, each developing different skills and strong friendships that remained with them for life. Now 21 years old, Maria had changed her name to Mary. She spent her time sewing clothes for the family and working as a seamstress at the clothing factory. Now known as Casper, 18-year-old Gaspare had a keen interest in electronics and communications. He taught himself Morse code and built radios to listen to communications between ships at sea from the third floor of their home. Gaspare also taught himself radio electronics by completing home study programs, and later in life, he became an electrician.[84] Luigi, now Louis, worked as a presser in a nearby clothing factory. Giovanni changed his name to John, Rosaria was now Rosanna, Anna (a.k.a. Annie), Giuseppe (a.k.a. George), and Alberto (a.k.a. Albert/Babe) were all listed in the 1910 U.S. census as attending school, while Florence was at home helping her mother.

---

xxv The reason is unknown, but Federal Census reports for all residential addresses that Giovanni lived at show that the di Bartolomeo surname was always the only Italian surname in the neighborhood.

In 1902, Maryland's compulsory education laws[85] required children to attend school until the age of 12. When the di Bartolomeo children attended school, an eighth-grade education was the standard. In the mid-Atlantic region of the United States, only 10% of the population graduated from high school.[86] High school attendance and graduation rates were lowest in areas most reliant on manufacturing. Due to Baltimore's abundance of jobs, high wages, and soaring industrial growth rates, education beyond the eighth grade was not highly valued. It wasn't until after 1930 that the mid-Atlantic regions saw a rapid expansion of high school graduation rates.

Due to the broad range of the di Bartolomeo children's ages, they attended different schools based on their location at the time. Maria graduated eighth grade in Jersey City. The 1910 census for their residence in Baltimore shows her working and not pursuing any other schooling. Gaspare attended first to eighth grade in Jersey City and may have attended night school in Baltimore, earning a high school equivalent, possibly at the Occupational Public School #28 located by their residence, which taught electrical and mechanical trades. The 1910 census shows Gaspare working as an electrician and not attending school.

Similarly, Louis attended first grade in Jersey City and graduated eighth grade in Baltimore. The 1910 census shows Louis working at the local clothing factory as a presser and not attending school at age 16. Anna attended first grade in Jersey City and graduated eighth grade in

Maryland, most likely at Thomas Johnson Public School or St. Mary, Star of the Sea. Both schools were located near their residence in Baltimore. George attended first to eighth grade in Baltimore, most likely at the same school, Thomas Johnson, then attended Baltimore City College, graduating in 1917. Albert attended the same schools in Baltimore for grades one to eight. In the 1930 census, Albert stated that he did not attend high school. When Albert was completing eighth grade, the economy in Baltimore was so strong that there was an insatiable demand for workers. The availability of good jobs with high pay prompted many students completing eighth grade to forego high school and go directly into the labor force or vocational training. Albert attended vocational school to learn stenography.[87] Florence, as the youngest, attended grades one to eight in Baltimore and most likely attended St. Joseph's School of Industry, which in 1926 was renamed Seton High School, located near their residence at Fenwick Avenue.[xxvi]

xxvi School building information is based on the homes' street location at the time (Jersey City and Baltimore 1896–1944 Sanborn Map); level of education is based on individuals' self-reporting in the Federal Census or draft registration, unless otherwise noted.

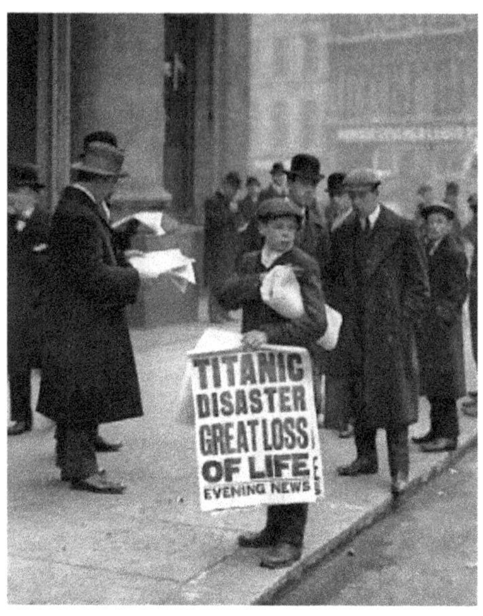

Newsboy April 15, 1912

Entertainment for families consisted mainly of dinner time storytelling, playing cards (Pitch), playing music, listening to the radio, and attending movies. Baltimore and other cities began to build large movie houses that seated over 1,000 people. The films were generally short compared to today's movies; 15-20 minutes. On April 15, 1912, Annie and her friends went to the local Echo Theater[xxvii] two blocks from their home on East Fort Avenue to watch a new film starring Lillian Gish and Lionel Barrymore. It was a recently released 17-minute classic musketeer swashbuckler produced by D.W. Griffith, *The Musketeers of Pig Alley*.

On that same day, news reached them that the Titanic had sunk.

xxvii In 1912, the Echo Theater located at 126 East Fort Avenue was the closest movie house to Anna's residence.

— CHAPTER SEVEN —

1905-1930

Family Life in Baltimore

McComas Street – Fort Avenue – South Charles Street

The Influence of the Roman Catholic Church

The di Bartolomeo home was always full of pleasant smells highlighted by traditional Abruzzo recipes the family had brought from Torre de' Passeri. Each region of Italy had its specific foods based on local growing conditions. Since Torre de' Passeri was in the Apennine Mountain region, a leg of spring lamb was for dinner whenever meat was on the menu. Vegetables of the Abruzzo region were eggplant, cauliflower, fava beans, and mushrooms. Traditional pasta was chitarra pasta made from durum wheat and eggs with no salt. During the holidays, there were traditional sweets—pizzelle, a cookie flavored with anise, and parrozzo, a cake dessert made from crushed almonds and chocolate.

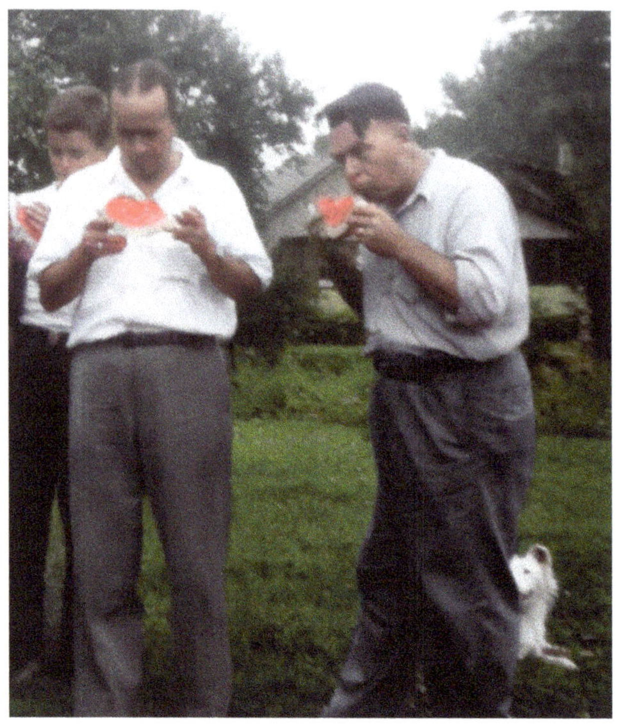

Brothers Albert and Louis enjoy watermelon, circa 1938

The family enjoyed their daily shopping at one of the four markets in the area. Several markets in the immediate area were Hanover Street Market, located two blocks from their home, Cross Street Market, a five-minute walk away, and Lexington Market or Broadway Market, located closer to Fells Point and Little Italy. The markets were the center of trade for Maryland farmers and importers bringing their goods up the Chesapeake Bay to Baltimore. The largest cash crops locally grown in Maryland where tomatoes, corn, and tobacco. Family farms dominated the land outside of the city. Baltimore's location on the Chesapeake Bay provided access to a rich source of seafood, including Maryland blue crabs, oysters, shad, and striped bass.

In his memoir, H.L. Mencken wrote that, in Baltimore, *"the food was incomparable and the women more beautiful and the citizens more honorable than anywhere on earth."* The 64,000-square-mile estuary, with its delicate balance of fresh and saltwater, was a significant source of food and recreation for the Baltimore area.

Fish Market - Smith and Faidley

Shoppers in the markets knew that they were in a world-class fish and seafood market when there was stall after stall of seafood and no evidence of the smell of fish. However, it was always easy to find the way to the seafood stalls by following the thin line of pale gray water slowly trickling down the aisle from the melting ice of the fishmongers' stalls. The biggest draws at the market were the oyster shuckers located directly across from the National Brewing Company's National Bohemian stall. Founded in

1855, the National Brewing Company established its brewery in Baltimore's Highlandtown neighborhood.[88]

As was the family's tradition, Giovanni made wine and often journeyed to the market searching for the best Montepulciano grapes. The village of Torre de' Passeri is the largest grower of Montepulciano grapes, not to be confused with Vino Nobile Montepulciano, a Tuscan wine made from Sangiovese grapes. George often accompanied Giovanni to the market to purchase crates of grapes for winemaking. The father and son's time at the market always took longer than anticipated. Usually, when they arrived home at the end of the day, George would have a story about his father's extended conversations with the merchants about the quality and providence of acquiring the plump, purple fruit.

The anticipated quarterly journey to the fruit market would commence with a casual walk north on Charles Street and then one block over onto East Pratt Street. The route to the market was always pleasant, providing views across the harbor and the salty smell of sea air mixed with the odor of industrial effluent from nearby factories. By the time Giovanni and George were two blocks from Water Street, they would see lines of hawkers and arabbers[xxviii] with horse carts loading fruit of every shape, size, color, and smell. The most aromatic fragrance was the rich sweetness of cantaloupe mixed with the pungent smell of the banana boats. Giovanni favored Vicari and Son or Jim Thompson Fruit companies for buying his

---

xxviii Independent street merchants in Baltimore who delivered fruit and produce from their brightly colored and decorated horse-drawn wagons; The Arabber Preservation Society.

grapes. Both family merchants had taken up stalls in the Centre Market, which had been in the same location in Baltimore since 1787. Giovanni preferred visiting Luigi Vicari and his son Giorgio on most market trips. The fruit market was enormous, with most of the merchants' stalls pushing out onto the street. Centre Market reached more than three blocks long, squeezed up against the harbor. The horizon was filled with dozens of ships anchoring in the port of Baltimore with fruit piled above the ship's transom bobbing up and down at the same rhythm of the frantic buzz of men moving fruit onto carts. Baltimore's six steamship companies provided access to international markets, and 13 coastal steamship companies gave access to the southern states, keeping harbor activity at a feverish pace 24 hours a day. The best show at the dock was the unloading of the great, white banana boat steamers carrying bananas from Cuba. Lumbering men with broad shoulders would form lines as the banana steamers pulled alongside the dock. Once the steamer docked, the long line of men would scramble up the plank at the stern and exit the bow with massive loads of bananas on their shoulders. They would carry out what looked to be whole trees of bananas, with each man heaving a load of at least 200. There were also large canvas sacks of coffee from Brazil, tobacco from South Carolina, and cantaloupes from Georgia.

To approach the produce stands, piled high with purple-stained wooden crates of grapes, Giovanni and George would have headed across the compressed, damp dirt floor with its intermittent grooves created by the wheels of pushcarts. Giovanni was always recognizable to merchants at the market by his brisk pace and ebullient half-smile in anticipation of the morning commerce. The fruit merchants enjoyed the pleasant but unnecessarily extended transaction, eventually seeing the 12 cents per pound grapes leave the market at 10 cents per pound. Both merchant and buyer anticipated the theatre of the purchase.

Baltimore Fruit Market - Vicari and Son

When Giovanni made wine, his plan included buying enough ingredients to make 48 bottles of wine, requiring 300 pounds of grapes, which involved the purchase of 25 wooden flats of prime fruit. Giovanni was known to carefully inspect every flat, looking for boxes that contained no twigs, no leaves, no green stems, and no crushed or slightly bruised fruit. The next step was the inspection of the grapes to look for firmness, deep purple color with a slight silver tint, referred to as "dusting," and plumpness. If the grapes were picked at their peak of freshness, deeply inhaling their aroma would reveal a nutty, peppery scent, indicating the fruit's readiness for winemaking. If grapes came from the same lot, Giovanni was assured of consistency in the quality of the fruit. After finishing a visual inspection, the final test every merchant objected to was pulling the grapes from the stems to test their release. The grape should release quickly from its pedicel[xxix] with just a pinch between the thumb and forefinger; no snap, no twist, no tug, no increased pressure beyond the experienced tweak. Otherwise, the indication is that the grapes were not ripe. A winemaker would consider the grapes' release carefully and would squeeze grapes across multiple flats, checking their firmness. The fruit merchant's amusing, animated fits of amazement would always reach their pinnacle when Giovanni grabbed two grapes and popped them into his mouth. He was looking for sweetness and administering his secret test—if the grapes were ready for winemaking, their pips would be chewable. No crunch, no snap in the mouth; just a soft press against the back right two molars should eviscerate the seed, releasing tannins and indicating that the fruit was worthy of its crusher.

Once the selection of fruit was complete, the merchant would load the boxes to be taken home to Giovanni's wine press. As the merchant turned to extract another flat to weigh, Giovanni would always add one cluster of grapes to each box, believing that he was overpaying based on the accuracy of the fruit broker's scale. The quarterly fruit market ritual

---

xxix Part of the stem that produces the initial bloom on the vine that becomes a grape.

followed the same process every time Giovanni made the trip to buy fruit for winemaking.

The acquisition of grapes would come to its familiar close with a handshake and a knowing nod from the merchant. Giuseppe would know from the merchant's passing glance that he had enjoyed his time with Giovanni as much as Giovanni had enjoyed being at his fruit stand. Then Giovanni would make arrangements with the fruit cart drivers outside the market to deliver the 300 pounds of grapes later in the day.

Their next stop after acquiring the grapes would be further west on Commerce Street to visit the butcher to purchase a lamb for dinner. A traditional Abruzzo favorite dinner was arrosticini. The dish was made from a castrated lamb, cut up into chunks, served with pane 'onde and Montepulciano d'Abruzzo wine. Not just any cut of lamb was acceptable. It had to be a "spring lamb," less than three months old, tender with rose-colored, sweet-tasting meat. A consensus regarding the spring lamb was usually reached between Giovanni and the butcher, but not until Giovanni had thoroughly questioned the merchants' family background and knowledge regarding the origin of a particular cut of lamb.[89] As a small business owner supporting a family of seven, Giovanni expected quality and value from others.

Market days with Giovanni were exhausting and usually required a commitment of half a day to acquire 300 pounds of grapes and two pounds of spring lamb. By accompanying his father on the many trips to the market, Giuseppe learned the importance of quality, thrift, and the value of maintaining lifelong relationships.

When Giovanni made wine, the process involved two pressings. For the first pressing, "the best wine," Giovanni and Giuseppe brought the boxes of ripe grapes home and loaded them into a fruit crusher, removed any remaining pulp from the crusher, and dumped them into a press. The grapes were pressed, the juice loaded into one of his four oak barrels, and yeast added for fermentation. Once fermentation was complete, the wine would be poured into bottles. The first pressing was reserved for special holidays or given to guests, particularly the local priests when they came to dinner. The second pressing involved reusing the remaining crushed grapes from the first crushing, filling the barrel with water, adding yeast, and letting it ferment. Once the fermentation process was complete, the wine was bottled. This process made good wine, slightly lighter than the first pressing's bright cherry color, and it would be consumed as the family's "everyday" wine.[90] Prohibition allowed 200 gallons of wine for personal and sacramental use, so winemaking continued uninterrupted in the di Bartolomeo family home.

The Influence of The Roman Catholic Church

Holy Rosary Catholic Church

The Catholic Church was the focal point of the community for Italian, Irish, and German immigrants. Particularly in Baltimore, where the Baltimore Roman Catholic Diocese was the first Catholic diocese founded in the United States in 1789, home of the first seminary in the U.S., St. Mary's Seminary established in 1791, and the first Catholic women's college, Notre Dame of Maryland, founded in 1895. Priests tended to be more highly educated than the general population, since they had received formal seminary training and could read and write English fluently. The church assisted immigrants with finding new homes and jobs. Catholic nuns supported families by instructing newly arrived children on English and local customs.

The di Bartolomeo children continued their religious education at St. Mary, Star of the Sea, while attending public school in Baltimore.[xxx] In

xxx The Baltimore Diocese has no records of the children attending school at St. Mary, Star of the Sea. Anna, Giuseppe, and Alberto did, however, receive their confirmation sacraments at St. Mary, Star of the Sea.

Interior of St. Mary, Star of the Sea, where Anna, George and Albert received Confirmation Sacrament

1914, St. Mary, Star of the Sea, built a new school building located at Battery Avenue and Giddings Street. The Sisters of St. Joseph taught classes at the new school. They were a congregation of sisters whose primary mission was educating students in Catholic schools, tutoring, and literacy programs.[91] The sisters also taught religion to students in the parish who attended public school. These were the same order of nuns that taught several of Giovanni's great-grandchildren 48 years later at St. Thomas More School in Baltimore.

New immigrants in America found spiritual comfort in familiar religious traditions and the numerous festivals held at the church. Along with the influx of Irish, Italians, and Poles, Catholicism in the U.S. was growing rapidly. In 1850, 5% of the U.S. population was Catholic. By 1906, due to the mass migration, the Catholic population had increased more than 300% to 17% of the U.S. population.

In addition to attending Mass at St. Mary, Star of the Sea, Giovanni also attended Mass at St. Leo's Roman Catholic Church located on Exeter Street in Baltimore's Little Italy.[92] Baltimore's Little Italy was the most popular destination for Italians migrating to Baltimore, and by 1920, the area was 100% Italian.

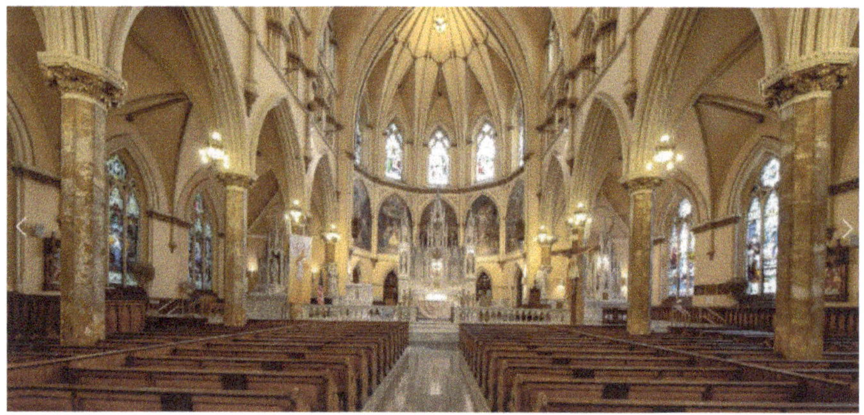

St. Patrick Roman Catholic Church – Jersey City, NJ, where Anna was baptized

Annie had received her sacrament of baptism at St. Patrick Roman Catholic Church in Jersey City, New Jersey, on April 24, 1898. Her godparents at the christening were her godfather, Antonio Napoleone, and her godmother, Frida Palauzio.[93] George was baptized at Chiesa Italiana Del Santissimo Rosario (Italian Church of the Most Holy Rosary) in Jersey City, New Jersey, by Father Federici. George's godfather was Giuseppe Janni (a.k.a. Yanni), and his godmother was Alfreda Varriano. The date of birth on George's baptismal certificate is February 23, 1899; however, in later years, George had modified this date to midnight, February 22.[94] Once he had adopted George as his first name, he thought it appropriate to reassign his birth by several hours to align with George Washington's birthday. On April 14, 1901, Alberto was baptized at Chiesa Italiana Del Santissimo Rosario (Italian Church of the Most Holy Rosary) in Jersey City, New Jersey. His godparents were Giuseppe Tomasetti and Elizabetta Lavigori. Father Vincenzo Sciolla was the officiant at the ceremony and baptized Alberto.[95] On June 20, 1909, Florence was baptized in St. Leo Parish[96] Catholic Church at 227 South Exeter Street in Baltimore. Florence's godparents were Joseph Castrilli and Agnes Schlick. Reverend O. di Paola officiated.[97]

St. Mary, Star of the Sea

Three of the children, Anna, George, and Albert, attended Mass and religious training at St. Mary, Star of the Sea,[98] where they received their sacraments of confirmation.[99] Based on dioceses records, Anna (age 13), George (age 11), and Albert (age 10) all received their confirmation sacraments at the same time at St. Mary, Star of the Sea, on December 18, 1910. The sacrament of confirmation for all three children at one time was a significant milestone event for the family and unusual due to the differences in their ages.

Records from the Star of the Sea state that George and Albert attended public school, and Anna attended religious training at the church's night school. Anna, was 13 at the time, so she had already completed her education in the eighth grade. The confirmation ceremony at St. Mary, Star of the Sea, was a remarkable event, with 330 individuals receiving the sacrament of confirmation, including 188 students from St. Mary, Star of the Sea, Catholic School, 74 from the local public school, 43 "workers," and 25 adults—night-class participants.[100]

The church played a decisive spiritual and social role in the families of immigrants and the di Bartolomeo family. Particularly in Italy, where there was limited or complete absence of a central government, leaving the Catholic Church as the only formal institution in the region. The universality of the church provided consistency across country and community borders. Entering into almost any Catholic church, parishioners felt that they were in a familiar setting. Mass unfolded in a consistent manner regardless of location. The typical cruciform architecture of churches and the church's role as a center of social activity provided a connection to the past, with religious festivals providing comfort to families that had left their ancestral homes behind.

No one does pageantry bigger or better than the Catholic Church. Growing up in a Catholic community, families attended dozens of sacramental Masses and witnessed the well-choreographed program accompanying the conveyance of sacraments. The delivery of sacraments was followed by festive celebrations that included extended family members and the local community.

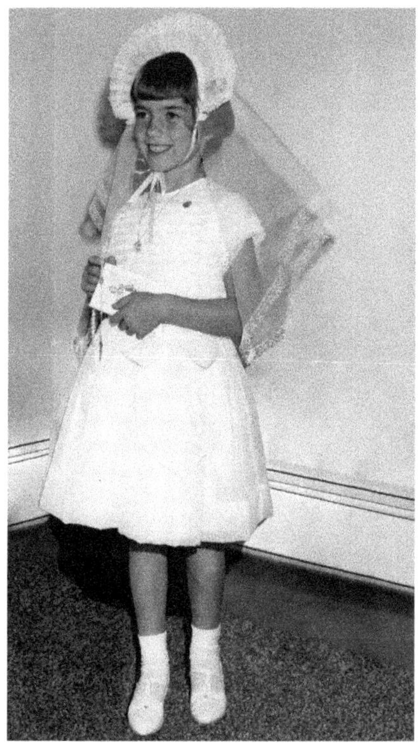

Rose Bartolomeo Brown, First Communion, circa 1964

By attending many First Communion Masses, all family members became familiar with the importance of the celebration to their family and the parish community. When entering the church, the first thing one noticed was the long center aisle intersected two-thirds of the way up towards the altar, creating the shape of the Latin cross that housed two naves, one on each end of the transepts. The symmetry of a Catholic church is impressive, with two pairs of confessional doors in the back, 14 Stations of the Cross, seven on each side, separated by stained glass windows, always tall with pointed arches except for the front of the church, which usually has a single, round-rose shaped stained glass window. The front of the church also has a semi-circular domed ceiling with a gold chancel lamp hanging over the altar, usually at the eastern end of the structure.

First Communion Mass

The families always arrived early for Mass, well before the usual start time. With synchronized precision, the nuns would emerge from the convent and organize long lines of boys and girls outside of the church. Once assembled, they'd deliver the signal to begin the process of entering the church.

The Eucharistic Mass, performed in Latin and as a Missa Canta, would begin with the organist in the loft proudly playing "Dona Nobis Pacem" on the foot-pumped Casavant reed organ. Altar boys dressed in white gowns would flat-footedly step down the center aisle with pure beeswax Paschal candles and crucifixes held high above their heads. They'd be followed by a row of deacons with hands folded in prayer, pointing straight up into the sky. As the Mass's celebrant entered, wearing a green Eucharistic chasuble with a mitre atop his head, he'd be preceded by a rising cloud of smoke and the smell of frankincense and myrrh embers. The clanging of the thurible would grow ever louder with the sound of the organ music. If the parish had the bishop lead the Mass, he'd carry his crosier, followed by a procession of girls dressed in white dresses, white knee socks, white closed-toe shoes, and veils on their heads. Behind them, the boys would proceed towards the altar, shoulder to shoulder in synchronized pairs, with the next row precisely three feet behind. The boys wore blue blazers and school ties in one primary color, either green, blue, or red, polished black shoes, and white armbands on their left arms, tied in a bow over the blazer at the center of the bicep. Now completed, the Mass would come to a close as the priest proceeded down the center aisle while the choir sang "Veni Creator Spiritus." The guests and proud grandparents, aunts, and uncles would all be beaming. Masses and parish celebrations were spiritual and social anchors for families.

Manresa; Louis is in fourth row under left pillar

In Baltimore, the Catholic Church established solid patriarchal roots initially based on the original Jesuit mission established in 1634[101] by Jesuit Fr. Andrew White in St. Mary's City, Maryland. With the assistance of Leonard Calvert, Lord Baltimore's brother, the Jesuits later expanded to the city of Baltimore establishing Jesuit-based institutions of higher learning that incorporated the spiritual direction of St. Ignatius of Loyola.

Father Griffith – seated, pastor of St. Bernard Church, George Bartolomeo, center

In addition to participating in the Catholic Church as children, Louis, George, and Albert were active in their local Parishes. Louis participated in annual spiritual retreats with the men from St. Rose of Lima. The Jesuit Retreat House, Manresa on the Severn, hosted men's groups for a week of reflection, spiritual reading, contemplation, Stations of the Cross, and celebration of Mass. Manresa on the Severn was founded in 1914 by The Society of Jesus, Jesuits of Maryland, holding its first retreat with 15 men from Georgetown University.

The Catholic Church provided meaningful social interactions for family life. George held leadership roles at St. Bernard Catholic Church, assisting the church to build a stronger foundation for men as the President of the Holy Name Society and Chairman of the St. Bernard's Executive Committee. The Holy Name Society, founded in 1274 as a confraternity for men, supports Catholic doctrine, the frequent reception of sacraments, and "Santissimo Nome di Gesù's" devotion to the holy name of Jesus. The St. Bernard's Holy Name Society held a weekly "For Men Only 8'o'clock Mass," a monthly father and son Mass, and encouraged participation in the Manresa Club. Albert was a leader at St. Dominic's Parish with the Knights of Columbus and a founder of The Knights "Cheese Club," a men's group that met every Friday to raise money for struggling parishes. While Albert was in the Knights of Columbus, "The Knights" Baltimore Council #205 chaired the "Orphans Santa Claus Party," providing Christmas cheer and a holiday meal for the orphans of Baltimore. All orphanages in the city attended the event, which was held every year on December 24th, filling Fords Theatre on West Fayette Street. The council put on an extravagant Christmas show with Santa Claus on stage and music provided by the St. Mary's Industrial School Band. Council members ensured that Santa had plenty of gifts for all the children. The council made a special effort to reunite orphan siblings who had been separated and lived at different orphanages[102] in the city.

Giovanni regularly attended Mass at St. Mary, Star of the Sea, in Locust Point and St. Leo's in Little Italy. In future years, most of Giovanni's grandchildren and great-grandchildren attended Baltimore area Catholic primary schools, high schools, and colleges, including St. Rose of Lima, St. Thomas More, St. Pius X, St. Mary of the Assumption, Mount St. Joseph, St. Dominic, St. Bernard, Loyola Blakefield, Loyola College, Institute of Notre Dame, and The Catholic High School of Baltimore.

Sister Siegberta (Maria), circa 1935

In June, 1910, Maria di Bartolomeo, now Mary Bartolomeo, applied to the Sisters of St. Francis of Philadelphia for admission to the convent. Maria entered the convent as a novitiate on August 23, 1910, and processed into the convent after completing her final vows as Sister M. Siegberta on July 7, 1913[103]. The convent in Philadelphia had 800 sisters, serving 88 missions in 19 dioceses, 12 hospitals, seven orphanages, and many elementary and secondary schools. At the age of 21, Maria, now known as Sister Siegberta,[xxxi] committed herself to a life of contemplation, poverty, and humility. The Sisters of St. Francis served the needs of others, especially the economically poor, the marginal, and the oppressed. Mary (Sister Siegberta) spent the rest of her life in service to others from the age of 21 at St. Mary's Convent in Bryn Mawr, Pennsylvania; Sacred Heart Convent in Allentown, Pennsylvania; and St. Francis Villa in Havre de Grace, Maryland;[104] until her death at the age of 64 on July 3, 1954.

---

xxxi Sister M. Siegberta became a naturalized citizen on April 14, 1946.

—— CHAPTER EIGHT ——

1915 - 1917

Lead-Up to WWI

Woodrow Wilson, a leader of the Progressive Movement,[105] had just been elected President of the United States. America's industrialization was accelerating, and change was underway, led by social activists and political reformers. In 1915, support for prohibition was increasingly gaining favor with Methodists and Baptists, and the U.S. House of Representatives eventually voted to reject giving women the right to vote. In Baltimore, suffragette protest and temperance parades were a regular occurrence. The first wave of efforts to support compulsory education was also underway for public schooling in response to the expansion of parochial schools. The rate at which Italian, Irish, and Polish children were graduating from eighth grade began to eclipse other nationalities due to the rapid growth of Catholic schools.[106] Higher education was also expanding, with the University of Maryland enrollment now at 500 and Johns Hopkins University expanding to its new campus in Homewood, the former estate of Charles Carroll, Jr., who was the son of Charles Carroll, a signer of the Declaration of Independence.

Wright aeroplane training in College Park, MD

In 1914, Germany, under the rule of Kaiser Wilhelm II, invaded Belgium, and in 1915, a German U-20 submarine sank the Lusitania off the coast of Ireland with 120 Americans onboard, who died, turning the tide of opinion in the U.S. against local Germans and Germany. In March of 1917, British intelligence made Woodrow Wilson aware of the "Zimmerman Telegram," proving that Germany had aggressively encouraged Mexico to wage war against the United States. The anti-German sentiment increased, and the U.S. entered the war on April 16, 1917. Baltimore felt the impact of rationing, and families were encouraged to plant "victory gardens" to support the war effort. Although bread, milk, and sugar were being rationed, the city continued to see increasing demand for labor and manufacturing to support the war effort. This continued growth in Baltimore and provided opportunities for the di Bartolomeo family. The area around Baltimore benefited from the construction and staffing of new federal wartime facilities. Camp Meade had recently been established, and during WWI, more than 400,000 new infantry recruits received their training there. The camp had also processed over 19,000 horses and mules to support the infantry in Europe. Aberdeen Proving Ground was another military facility constructed just north of the city to build and test munitions and ordnances. Less than one mile from the di Bartolomeo family's home, Fort McHenry was also reactivated. In 1917, Fort McHenry experienced rapid reconstruction and served as an Army hospital. The facility provided 3,000 beds and specialized as a surgical center for facial reconstruction.

In Dundalk, Maryland, Fort Holabird opened as a military transport center for Detroit-made vehicles and trained soldiers to drive and repair them.

Meanwhile, 30 miles away in College Park, Maryland, Wilbur Wright trained new military pilots to fly airplanes.[107] Automakers were rapidly changing their vehicle-production lines to manufacture military transportation. The war ended with Germany signing the Armistice of Compiegne on November 11, 1918, only 18 months after the U.S. declared war on Germany in 1917. When WWI ended after less than two years, U.S. auto manufacturers were caught unprepared by the quick end to the war. It took them a year to retool for consumer vehicles, hire new workers, and establish contracts with parts suppliers to increase

George Bartolomeo with Ford Model T, circa 1930

production and meet post-war demand. Heading into 1920, production of the Ford Model T was back at full operating capacity, and Baltimore's industrial complex was again rapidly expanding.

—— CHAPTER NINE ——

1920

Federal Hill and Move to South Charles Street

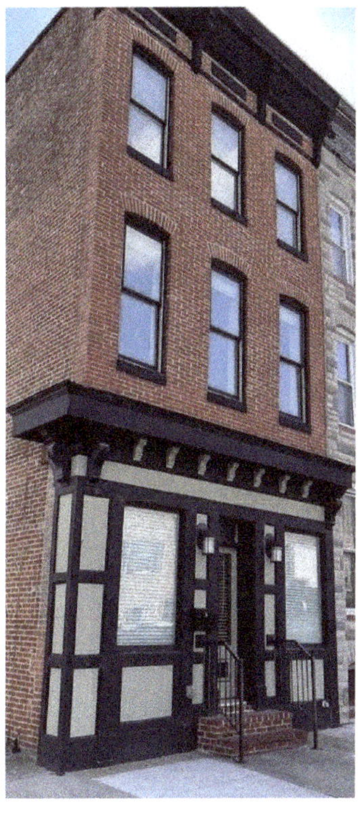

1501 South Charles Street

Sometime before 1920, as Giovanni continued to grow his business, he moved the family from the Fort Avenue house and relocated to a much larger home at 1501 South Charles Street,[108] located six blocks north in the Federal Hill section of Baltimore. The homes located in the Charles Street neighborhood were designed in the Federal style; tall, stately, and constructed from brick. The end-corner row homes were almost always three stories tall, 18 feet wide, and two rooms deep. The extra space permitted street-level egress for trade and retail. The second-floor level housed the family living quarters, and the third floor was for sleeping. Giovanni's home at 1501 South Charles Street was set up in this manner, allowing the first-floor level to serve as the storefront for his shoemaking business.

Baltimore's historic Federal Hill neighborhood is elevated 46 feet above the Baltimore harbor on the north branch of the Patapsco River. During the revolutionary war period, the land under Federal Hill was excavated to mine pigments for dye and paint. In the early 1800s, and due to Federal Hill's location near the harbor, the business community increased, and the area became a hub for shipbuilding. By the late 1800s, the 46-foot rise served as a signaling hill alerting people of ships arriving with passengers and goods from around the world.

Baltimore was famous for its uniform city blocks of red brick row homes. Throughout the diverse neighborhoods, regardless of their style, Federal, Artistic, Italianate, Daylight, or Postwar, they had a marble stoop, sometimes a covered porch, and were always made of brick.

Before 1850, the bricks used to build the row houses were made from a clay mixture with a high sand content; they were salmon colored and not uniform in size. Because of the high sand content, the bricks were porous, which led to the erosion of homes' facades and eventually required people to paint the brick homes to preserve their structure. In 1850, a new and better method of brickmaking emerged. The process, performed by hand, entailed compressing the sand, clay, and water mixture in an 8" x 3 5/8" x 2 1/4" shaped form press. Pressing the bricks in this way minimized the pores in the brick and provided for a consistent shape that allowed for uniform mortar joints. The bricks used for post-1850 row homes originated mainly from the Baltimore Brick Company. The Baltimore Brick Company operated a foundry on East Monument Street, where the clay bricks were kiln fired.[109]

Caring for Baltimore's famous marble steps

Unlike row homes in other cities, Baltimore row homes did not have an English basement, which consisted of an elevated front entrance eight to 10 feet above the street and a basement entrance below street level under the front steps. Baltimore row homes were only slightly elevated but provided a two-foot rise above street level to maintain privacy in the house from people passing on the road. The home's front entrance was approached by ascending two to three marble steps. The steps were built using three stacked white marble slabs with a rise of 7 ½ inches, step run of 10 inches, and nosing of ¾ inches, and they were bright white with soft, dove-colored veins highlighting the beauty of the stone. The marble used for steps in Baltimore rowhouses was mined from a local Maryland quarry in Cockeysville, Maryland. This same marble was used for building the 555-foot-tall Washington Monument obelisk located on the Mall in Washington, D.C.[110] Baltimore's Preservation Society estimates that 60% of all marble steps in Baltimore are from marble mined at the Beaver Dam quarry in Cockeysville. Once the quarry was closed, its walls were squared, concreted on the sides, and the deep quarry holes filled with water. The owners turned the quarry into a popular swim club with live music. Many Baltimoreans learned to swim in the repurposed quarries at Beaver Dam and Beaver Springs in the '50s and '60s, including Giovanni's future great-grandchildren.

The row houses' marble steps were highly prized and a great source of pride and tradition in Baltimore.[111] To maintain the marble's polished beauty, residents would spend an hour every Saturday scrubbing the steps with soapstone, steel wool, and pumice. H.L. Menken, a Baltimore essayist and writer for *The Baltimore Sun*, commented, *"Some people in recent times have gone so far as to paint their marble trim, an obscenity perhaps unmatched in Christendom."*

—— CHAPTER TEN ——

1915 - 1931

Giovanni and Rosaria's Children Start Their Own Families Anti-Immigration Sentiment in The U.S. 1920

"You can't do anything about the length of your life, but you can do something about its width and depth."

—— H. L. Mencken

The lead-up to 1920 after the war provided a dynamic economic background that drove ample opportunity and economic growth. The family grew with it. Giovanni and Rosaria's children had all taken advantage of favorable conditions for education and training to become respected, skilled tradespeople or by seizing on positions with companies in high-growth industries. Their personal growth led to upward mobility and provided the foundation for Casper, Louis, Anna, George, Albert, and Florence to become independent and start their own families.

After 20 years in the United States, family members had fully assimilated and became "Americans." Along with becoming independent adults and establishing their own identities as heads of their families, other changes occurred. The di Bartolomeo last name became Bartolomeo to simplify pronunciation and reflect a more modern surname convention. However, Giovanni maintained the di Bartolomeo surname until his passing in 1937.

The "di" prefix naming convention is a "patronymic," which means that the surname is derived from the name of the individual's father. The "di" patronymic was almost exclusively used by Abruzzo, Molise, and Sicilian families. This naming convention was started in Europe during the mid-1500s when it became a requirement to register both the individual's first name and last name. Before that, early Europeans were known either by their geographic origin or profession, for example, John Baker was a baker, or in the example of Leonardo Da Vinci, the use of the Da meant that he was Leonardo from Vinci. The "di" patronymic reflected that you were Giovanni "of the" Bartolomeo family. It was no longer necessary, so most families dropped the di.

The family members also changed their first names to conform and simplify pronunciation. By 1905, all family members had anglicized their first names. Giovanni had dropped Giovanni and replaced it with John, Rosaria with Rose, Maria with Mary, Gaspare with Casper, Luigi with Louis, Anna with Annie, Giuseppe with George, Alberto with Albert, and in 1908, Florentina with Florence.

While the Americanized first names appeared for the first time in 1905, it was not until the children left Giovanni and Rosaria's home that they began using "Bartolomeo" exclusively as their legal surname; Louis in 1915, Anna in 1919, Casper in 1921, George in 1927, Albert in 1928, and Florence in 1931.

Between 1915 and 1931, America experienced historic changes impacting politics, science, and entertainment. Author F. Scott Fitzgerald published *The Great Gatsby*, NBC and CBS established the first national radio networks, and Charles Lindberg made the first transatlantic flight. In 1919, women obtained the right to vote; in 1915, transatlantic telephone service was launched, and following Maria's departure to the convent in 1910, Louis Bartolomeo was the next of Giovanni's children to journey out on their own.

LOUIS BARTOLOMEO

Julia and Louis Bartolomeo with sons Earl and Roy, circa 1928

At age 21, Luigi, known as Louis L. Bartolomeo, was working as a machinist in the armature industry.[112] As a teenager, he had held several positions, including jobs as a garment presser for a clothing factory at age 16 and cabinet maker at the age of 19.[113] He purchased a home outside Baltimore at 115 Annapolis Boulevard, Brooklyn Park, Maryland, located in Anne Arundel County.[114] Louis married Julia Rowland on June 13, 1915. Their wedding was held at the family's church, St. Mary, Star of the Sea. The church marriage records state that Louis di Bartolomeo was born in Rome, Italy *[sic]*. Hannah Floyd and Kati Rowland witnessed the marriage, and Father Francis Flannigan officiated the wedding.[115] In 1917, Louis registered for the draft while employed by Bartlett & Heyward Metal Working Foundry.[116]At the time, it was the largest iron foundry in the U.S. Bartlett and Heyward's foundry operated in the Pigtown section of Baltimore, so named for the number of butcher shops and livestock pens, and in later years, the storage of pig iron. Pigtown was also the neighborhood in Baltimore where Babe Ruth grew up and attended St. Mary's Industrial School, later to become Cardinal Gibbons School.

Julia in background, Earl front (L), Roy front (R), Louis (right side middle of table), circa 1939

Before WWI, Bartlett & Heyward manufactured iron gas fixtures, railroad engines, and machine pistons. The foundry produced metal castings made from sand molds, later filled with liquefied steel to make metal parts. The foundry employed skilled pattern makers to create the molds, core makers, metal pourers, and grinders. During WWI, the Bartlett & Heyward Company converted their foundry to produce munitions, artillery cartridges, ships propellers, and ammunition cartridges. Their first large wartime order was to supply 750,000 artillery shells for American allies fighting in Europe. Louis worked as a "three-inch munitions" assembler.[117] Military contracts increased their employment from 4,000 to 22,000 workers. In 1917, they produced 20,000 shells per day at their Turner Station facility in Sparrows Point.[118] On April 5, 1917, Louis's draft registration indicated that he was married, living at 1634 Light Street, employed by Bartlett & Heyward, and born in New York, N.Y. *[sic.]*.

In later life, Louis became a carpenter. After registering for WWII in 1942, he worked for the W.M. C. Scherer Company, a woodworking and cooperage company located in Baltimore at 1108 West Baltimore Street.[119] Louis and Julia were living in their new home at 4105 Ritchie Highway with their children John (1917–1993), Roy (1923–1965), Earl (1924–2011) and Rosemary (1927–2011).

Louis was a highly skilled carpenter and a member of Carpenters Union Local #974. He was capable of building almost anything, from fine furniture and cabinets to a complete home. Louis became a naturalized citizen of the United States of America on September 10, 1945. His Certificate of Naturalization shows that he was at the time a widower, having lost his wife Julia, and that two fingers on his right hand were short.[120]

Anna Bartolomeo, the granddaughter of Louis and Julia, recalls the stories that her father Earl shared with her at their dinner table. Earl told Anna that as a child, *"they spent Sundays at Giovanni and Rosaria's home enjoying Sunday dinners and playing cards in the evening."* He also said that *"Rosaria was a quiet woman, likely because of her limited ability to speak English. Rosaria did, however, always have Good 'n Plenty candies in her apron to share with the children."*

Louis and his older brother, Casper, spent many days building the family's shore home, originally located at Brandon Shores on the Patapsco River. The "shore" was the family's center of activity, favorite family summer residence, and weekend retreat to host relatives and friends from Baltimore.

Left to right: John, Unknown, Louis, Roy, Julia at the beach, circa 1929

After several years, the family decided to move the structure of the original shore house in Brandon Shores to a location 1.5 miles away in Orchard Beach. The new site for the home was at the mouth of Patapsco Bay on Stoney Creek and the Patapsco River. With broad panoramic views across the river and out to the Chesapeake Bay, the property is where everyone enjoyed swimming, fishing, and crabbing. Anna recalls family stories that this is where *"Louis taught everyone to swim at an early age."* With no indoor toilet, there was an outhouse in the backyard under a mulberry tree, where everyone who ventured to the outhouse acquired "purple feet." The house and pier were damaged by storms several times throughout its history. After one storm had caused significant damage to the property, Louis rebuilt the shore house, adding an indoor toilet and eliminating purple feet.

Louis was known for his enjoyment of time with his family, many close friends, and generosity. He accompanied his friends who had a band, and he often joined them on Saturday nights when they were playing around the area at local political events, crab feasts, and bull and oyster roasts. When he learned that his daughter Rosemary wanted her own hairdressing business, Louis built her a beauty salon in the front of the house.

Louis at the microphone with band, Esther, behind Louis, at Esther and John's (Louis's son) house on Annabel Avenue

On July 31, 1960, Louis passed away while spending time with friends, family, and grandchildren at the shore home. Louis greatly valued family and the time spent with his grandchildren. After Louis had passed and his sons were clearing out his house in Brooklyn Park, Maryland, they found Christmas envelopes Louis had already addressed to each grandchild with money inside. Even though he had passed six months before Christmas, everyone still received a Christmas gift from Louis.

Louis was gifted, and as a skilled tradesman, he was most like his father, Giovanni. The talent and drive to develop and follow detailed plans defined him as an accomplished craftsman. He worked with his hands to create extraordinary results from raw materials. Louis found great pleasure in building a retreat at the shore, combining his passion for his craft and family.

The family always had fond memories of their summers with Louis at the shore.

ANNA BARTOLOMEO PFEIFER

Anna Bartolomeo Pfeifer, circa 1940

Anna was the first child of Giovanni and Rosaria to be born in the U.S. Anna was known as Annie during most of her childhood. The week before Easter in 1919, at the age of 21, she married August Pfeifer on Wednesday, April 9.[121] The civil ceremony[xxxii] took place in Alexandria, Virginia. Anna and Gus met at one of the weekly Friday night dances

xxxii The marriage records list them both as 21. Anna as born in Jersey City, parents listed as Rose and John. August is listed as born in Baltimore, son of Conrad and Caroline.

regularly held at St. Mary, Star of the Sea.[122] August was a member of the Holy Cross boys' chorus. The boys' chorus from Holy Cross Church performed at the Friday night dance on the evening Anna and August met. Holy Cross School was the oldest Catholic school on Federal Hill and was founded to serve the area's dominant German population.

Anna and August initially resided at 2709 Fenwick Avenue with August's brother-in-law, Joseph Sauter, and August's sister, Mamie.[123] Based on an interview recorded in 1984 with Anna Bartolomeo Pfeifer, she and August eloped and were married in Alexandria, Virginia. Anna and August returned to Baltimore the following week for Easter dinner with the Bartolomeo family, where Giovanni met them for the first time after the elopement. Giovanni shook hands with August and hugged Anna. August and Anna were the first generation of Americans in their respective families to be married and start a new family in the United States. August's parents were born in Germany and Anna's in Italy.

Anna and August's first child was Madalyn Rita Pfeifer, born November 6, 1919, in Baltimore, Maryland.[124] Between 1921 and 1925, the United States experienced an epidemic outbreak of diphtheria, which caused the death of 206,000 people. Earl Lederle, the former New York City Health Commissioner who started Lederle Laboratories, had invented an anti-toxin for diphtheria for adults. Still, it wasn't until 1930 that diphtheria vaccines were widely available for children. By 1940, diphtheria vaccines had become compulsory and were combined into a single vaccine with tetanus and pertussis vaccines.

A sorrowful event occurred on December 27, 1922, when Madalyn, at the age of three years and one month, died from diphtheria and myocarditis. Madalyn passed away on that date at 3 a.m. Funeral services were held at the parents' residence located on Annapolis Boulevard, in Brooklyn Park, Maryland, the next day. Madalyn was laid to rest at Most Holy Redeemer Cemetery.

Anna and August received comfort and support from Anna's brothers and sisters. At that time, they were living next door to Louis and Julia. They continued to be resilient parents, raising their two children, Frances and Duane.

In later years, Anna remained excited and enthusiastic, becoming a big part of her grandchildren's lives. Known as Nana, her grandchildren loved her dearly. Nana was the center of attention for Sunday dinners, holidays, overnight babysitting, and occasional weekend excursions. Slightly introverted and private, Anna allowed others to take the stage while observing activities at the large family gatherings. Sunday dinners with Nana were steaming pots of pasta accompanied by the sweet smells of tomato sauce at her brick row home at 1617 East 24th Street, where the children explored the mysteries and treasures of the cellar. Deborah Pfeifer Morrissey, one of Anna's granddaughters, recalls that the favorite attraction in the basement was riding around the floor on a bright red Pump and Go go-cart. The driver of the vehicle would sit on the sleek, flat, sheet metal iron cart, brace their legs against the frame at the front of the cart, and pump the handles back and forth as hard as possible while steering at the same time. After exhausting the arms, shoulders, and legs on the cart ride, there were always Dad's military service memorabilia, which Anna's grandson Duane, known as Duey, enjoyed rummaging through, and Pop Pop's violin to explore.

When the grandchildren's parents attended late-night festivities with friends, New Year's Eve became an annual opportunity for sleepovers at Nana's. Nana enjoyed the late nights with her granddaughters, coloring with the newly acquired 32-pack of Crayola crayons and advising the girls on the latest fashions and pop culture. The evenings always ended with Nana leading the grandchildren in the loud banging of pots and pans at midnight, watching the rogue neighborhood fireworks, and singing.

Anna followed the latest fashions closely, and when Audrey Hepburn appeared with bangs for her latest hairstyle, Anna knew that *they*, the fashion insiders, were "going bangs," so she announced to the girls, "They are going bangs." She loved to observe her grandchildren and plan adventures with them. Around the summer of 1957, Anna decided that it was time to take a weekend girls' trip to one of her favorite destinations with her two granddaughters, Deborah and Bonnie. Anna, age 60, sisters Deborah and Bonnie, between eight and 10 years of age, boarded a Greyhound bus at the West Baltimore Street terminal at 9 a.m. for Atlantic City, New Jersey. The silver and white Greyhound "Scenic Cruiser," with a bright blue painted front and a large greyhound dog running down its side panels carried the trio on their three-day adventure. The bus arrived in Atlantic City at 12:45 after three hours and 45 minutes. Until the

1960s, when inexpensive airfare made travel to Florida affordable, Atlantic City was the most popular beach destination for people in the Northeast. In its heyday between 1930 and 1960, Atlantic City was an adult playground, hosting famous entertainers like Frank Sinatra, Bing Crosby, and Bill Haley and the Comets. There was also the renowned nightlife at the Jockey and 500 clubs. During this trip with Nana, the granddaughters were treated to walks on the five-mile-long boardwalk, exhibits, and games. Seeing the latest innovation from General Motors and making a voice recording of the two girls and grandmother singing were highlights of the trip.

America was closing out the 1950s period of innocence, and the coming decade of the '60s was already beginning to impact fashion. The age of the "Mad Men" of Madison Avenue advertising was taking hold, promoting everything with style and flair. Anna knew that *they*, the fashion insiders, were going bleached blonde, and this was something that her granddaughter needed to experience. Deborah Pfeifer Morrissey recalls that Nana had Bonnie's hair bleached blonde during their weekend in Atlantic City. "Why not?" proclaimed Nana, "they're going blonde this year," and her girls needed to be part of the trend. All three considered the weekend in Atlantic City a raging success. The girls returned home happy and excited. On arrival in Baltimore to meet their mother, Mom was not happy.

The Pump and Go go-cart became scarred with rust-colored lines across its shiny white wheels, and the hard rubber tires became slick from the thousands of trips across the linoleum basement floor. Hair colors changed many times. Memories of the road trip with Nana remain vivid.

Anna and August resided at 1617 East 24th Street with their two children, Frances (1922–1981) and Duane (1925–2003), until August's death in 1952.[125] After several years, Anna moved to be closer to her daughter Frances on 36th Street across from Memorial Stadium.

When Anna moved to the stadium area, sports teams in Baltimore were attracting large crowds. Anna's grandchildren were also enthusiastic fans. In 1970, the Orioles won the American League East and had an all-star team that included Brooks Robinson, Frank Robinson, Dave McNally, Mark Belanger, Davey Johnson, and Paul Blair. The Orioles appeared in three World Series between 1969 and 1971.

Also in 1971, the Baltimore Colts, led by Earl Morrall, who came in for an injured Johnny Unitas, defeated the Dallas Cowboys to win the 1970 season NFL Superbowl.

Another advantage of living in the brick row home across the street from the stadium was that the front lawn and rooftop provided a gathering spot for family members to watch fireworks on the Fourth of July.

Duey Pfeifer recalls that they would visit his grandmother Anna after baseball games. For Anna, family was synonymous with food, so she always prepared a post-game feast of spaghetti and meatballs for Duey and his friends, no matter how much they pleaded to Anna about the number of hot dogs they had consumed during the game.

Being close to the stadium did have its drawback. In addition to crowds and congestion, there were night games at Memorial Stadium. In an interview with Anna's daughter Frances Pfeifer McKittrick, *The Baltimore Sun* reported on October 10, 1970, "*Frances McKittrick stood on her front porch watching her husband and son. 'There is some litter after the games, though more from Colt games than Oriole games, and stadium lights are so bright that you can read a newspaper in the bedroom with the drapes closed.'*"

The grandchildren loved the Colts, Orioles, and their Nana.

Later in her life, Anna lived with her son Duane and his wife, Margaret, in St. Michaels, and Peachtree City, Georgia, until her passing on February 22, 1994. Anna and August are interred at Most Holy Redeemer Cemetery.

As Giovanni and Rosaria's firstborn in America, Anna had no preconceptions of life as an Italian immigrant and celebrated her life as a modern young lady. Anna lived life intensely, and her fondness for music, fashion, and style were only second to her adoration for her family.

Anti-Immigration and Anti-Catholic Sentiment in the United States (1920)

Anti-immigration sentiment began to build in 1920. Southern Europeans and Italians, in particular, were impacted, since they were the largest group to have migrated to the U.S. in the 1900s. Several events led to this sentiment. Propagandists appealed to Protestants and portrayed Italians as insular, prone to crime, and ignorant of democracy. By the 1920s, self-proclaimed "experts" were advancing the notion that Italians were a separate race from Anglo-Americans, and the federal government established immigration quotas for southern Europe to reduce immigration from Italy. In 1921, the U.S. government passed the Emergency Quota Act that restricted open immigration and reduced the number of most nationalities coming into the U.S. The government set quotas for each ethnicity based on 3% of the immigrant population listed in the 1910 census. The government established the Dillingham Commission to study the impact of immigrants coming to the U.S.[126] The commission adopted a belief in eugenics, stating that "certain bad traits" were inherent in some nationalities. The commission also distinguished between "old immigrants," defined as Northern and Western European, and "new immigrants," defined as Southern European and Asian immigrants. The commission claimed that the new immigrants were less progressive than the "old" immigrants and did not assimilate into American society.

Additionally, they identified nationalities such as the Polish, stating that their physical features were much more "Slavic" than Northern European, thereby prejudicially reducing their future immigration numbers. Anti-immigration sentiment continued to increase as nativism, the belief that mental capacity was innate, not learned, grew in the U.S. Additional legislation was enacted in 1924, further reducing quotas for Southern Europeans and Asians.

Babe Ruth Raps Un-American, Anti-Private School Bill

Had it not been for a private industrial school he never would have been heard of, declared Babe Ruth, famous baseball player, in discussing Initiative No. 49, during his brief visit to Seattle last Saturday. St. Mary's Catholic Industrial School, taught by Catholic Brothers and supported by the charitably inclined Catholic people of the Baltimore Archdiocese, was the only home the "Bambino" knew in his boyhood and to St. Mary's he asserts he owes all he is. Even his knowledge of baseball was taught him by one of the brothers. He expressed the hope that the un-American anti-private school measure would be decisively defeated.

Catholic NW Progress October 24, 1924

Catholicism had also come under attack. Particularly in Italian parishes where the Italian brand of Catholicism was being blended with what some people believed were pre-Christian rituals, such as festivals and celebrations that included parades for saints creating a "cult of saints"[127] for the uneducated and superstitious Catholic immigrants. To raise the education level of immigrant children, Catholic parishes began building parochial schools. The expanded educational opportunity for the poor and marginalized immigrant children threatened the existing status of who was permitted to attend school and how individuals received a quality education previously reserved for more affluent white Protestants. The most public threat was from the Ku Klux Klan,[128] which championed "only people like them were capable of becoming real Americans." They had legislation added to the ballot, "initiative 49," which was later thrown out by the Supreme Court, that banned children from attending Catholic schools.[129] The Klan created fear in the general population, promoting the idea that neighborhoods were under siege by Catholic immigrants. Selling themselves to the public as a law enforcement organization,[130] the Klan seized on prohibition[131] as a way for Klan members to enter immigrants' homes and terrorize the occupants. The third element that created the xenophobic backlash was hiring Italian immigrants to fill positions when American workers went on strike, inciting further rage against Italians.

CASPER BARTOLOMEO

Casper and Cecelia Lawrence (Bartolomeo)

Casper was born Gaspare di Bartolomeo in Torre de' Passeri, Italy, via San Vittorino on July 7, 1892. His birth was reported by Giovanni di Bartolomeo on July 11, 1892,[132] and recorded in the Torre de' Passeri civil records by Francesco di Vingalia. Casper arrived from Italy to Ellis Island on January 12, 1897, with travel ticket number 26. His name was accurately recorded on arrival as Gaspare di Bartolomeo by the Purser of the S.S. Werra, Augusta Kolhnsen.

At the age of 25, Gaspare di Bartolomeo continued to build on his self-taught knowledge of electronics and worked as an electrician for eight years before the United States entered WWI. On October 11, 1917, he enlisted in the army and served as an electronics specialist and Morse code instructor[133] at Camp Meade, located 20 miles south of Baltimore.

Morse code communications training for new WWI recruits – Camp Meade, circa 1917

After the war, on January 13, 1920, the U.S. Federal Census shows that Gaspare resided with Giovanni and Rosaria at 1501 South Charles Street and worked as an electrician at Camp Meade. In 1921, he moved to Wheeling, West Virginia, and started the C.B. Lawrence Electric Company.[134] On November 27, 1936, according to social security registration records, Gaspare di Bartolomeo changed his name to Casper

Bartholomew Lawrence, born in Jersey City, New Jersey, son of John D. Lawrence and Rosanna L. Bartholomew.[135] He married Cecelia Bradbury in 1923 and had sons Robert in 1929 and Donald in 1936. Casper and Cecelia's engagement was announced in *The Pittsburgh Press* on July 1, 1923, and their wedding was reported in *The Cincinnati Enquirer* on July 8, 1923. The 1930 census and 1942 WWII draft registration show that Casper was renting a home with his wife and one-year-old son at 84 12th Street in Wheeling, West Virginia, and working for the C.B. Lawrence Electric Company. The 1940 census shows that he owned his home located at 25 Locust Avenue in Wheeling, was employed as an electrical contractor, had a college education,[xxxiii] and earned $3,600 in 1940.[136]

Due to growing nativism, anti-immigration sentiment, and new legislation to control the migration of Southern Europeans to the United States, Casper decided to make a change. He did not want his opportunity to be limited based on changing social sentiment about immigrants. Casper remade himself into an image of what the general population believed an ideal American to be. To do this, he created a new persona,[xxxiv] C.B. Lawrence, who was born in New Jersey to American parents, a patriot and a veteran of WWI, a skilled tradesman, and a successful businessperson. During this period of his life, Casper and his family stayed in touch with members of the Bartolomeo family, traveling with

xxxiii There were no records located to document and confirm Casper attending college.

xxxiv There are no records available that Casper filed a Declaration of Intent of Naturalization or applied for citizenship. Since he maintained that he was a natural-born U.S. citizen, filing a declaration seemed unnecessary to Gaspare.

his family from West Virginia and often visiting during holidays and family events.[137]

Casper's wife Cecelia was born in Wheeling, West Virginia, on March 15, 1898. She passed away in March, 1982. On October 8, 1973, Casper died at Fairview General Hospital in Cleveland, Ohio.

GEORGE BARTOLOMEO

George Bartolomeo, circa 1920

Upon graduating from Baltimore City College, on September 12, 1918, George registered for the military draft. He registered as George Joseph Bartolomeo and submitted his date of birth as "midnight," February 22,[138] rather than February 23, to coincide with George Washington's birthday. The military draft registration described George as 5'6" tall, 135 lbs., with dark brown eyes and black hair.[139]

Twelve years prior, in 1905, at the age of five, Giuseppe di Bartolomeo boarded a train in Jersey City for Baltimore. He was now in the final years of his education in America as George Joseph Bartolomeo.

In 1917, only a small portion of the population was attending high school. In the mid-Atlantic region of the United States, less than 19% of the population attended and graduated from high school. Less than half of 1% attended and graduated from college. Graduating from high school in 1917 was a rare achievement for a first-generation American and son of a shoemaker and farmer. Giovanni had been so fascinated by the level of education that George was getting that he thought George would one day become a professor.[140]

Baltimore continued to prosper as a major center of commerce, and Baltimore business owners demanded a public high school that would meet their needs by educating young men. In 1839, the City founded Baltimore City College, and they established the first campus on Courtland Street. In 1873 a fire destroyed the Courtland Street campus, and the City developed the new campus on North Howard and Centre Streets. The campus continued to experience setbacks due to the rapid development in the immediate area. In 1892, the building collapsed due to the excavation for a tunnel by the B&O railroad under the campus structure. The school then moved to an annex across the street where George Bartolomeo attended classes for four years and graduated.

After World War One, there was increased demand for high school education. The City expanded the campus to accommodate the need for a high school that specialized in college preparatory curriculum. In 1926, the City erected the iconic Baltimore City College Tower, which became a national historic landmark.

Baltimore City College was an imposing structure. At first sight, you'd believe that you were looking at a castle on a hill. That was the first impression looking up from the corner of Centre and Howard Streets towards Baltimore City College. The gothic center tower stood 150 feet tall and dominated the Baltimore skyline—earning the college the nickname "The Castle on the Hill." The view from the tower was spectacular. To the south was the thriving harbor; to the west stood St. Joseph's Industrial High School (Seton High School); to the east and north, a view of Johns Hopkins. On the way to work, local commuters would have noticed dozens of young men 14–18 years of age headed to the school, carrying books and dressed in suits complemented by starched, removable collars.

Baltimore City College (rebuilt in 1926 and opened in 1928)

Baltimore City College, founded as an International Baccalaureate High School for grades nine to 12, was the third-oldest high school in the U.S. The school's mission was to prepare its students to succeed at the best colleges in the U.S. Their educational program was so rigorous that Johns Hopkins permitted graduating students to enroll at the university without taking the entrance exam.[141] Students at Baltimore City College selected one of two academic tracks. They chose either Liberal Arts, Humanities, and the Classics; or Science, Math and Technology. Their athletic teams competed in the college division with regular-season football games against the United States Naval Academy, St. John's University, the University of Maryland, and Swarthmore. Baltimore City College vs. Baltimore Polytechnic High School is also the oldest high school rivalry in the United States. On Thanksgiving Day every year, Poly played City in the afternoon, and Loyola High School played Calvert Hall in the morning. The alumni of Baltimore City College included future business leaders such as Charles McCormick, literary scion Russell Baker, three Congressional Medal of Honor recipients, and numerous future governors of the State of Maryland.[142] Circa 1917, George (Giuseppe) di Bartolomeo was in his fourth year at Baltimore City College and enjoyed academic challenges and attending the weekly football games with his friends.

George Bartolomeo attending class at Baltimore City College 1917, seated far rear corner

He and his friends respected the school's slogan, PALMAM QUI MERUIT FERAT, "Let whoever earns the palm bear it." The expression reflects the significance of palms as a symbol of triumph and victory, by holding fast to self-reliance, and references the Roman custom of giving the victorious gladiator a palm branch as a reward for his prowess.

Following graduation from high school, George took a position with the Calvert Stove and Heating Company in 1918.[143] The 1920s began an era of innovation for residential heating and kitchen appliances. Most homes used a single source of fuel, either coal or wood, for both heating and cooking. World War I increased the demand for coal, creating a shortage of coal for residential use. This opened the door for innovation in the home using natural gas. Innovation for kitchen ovens entailed the introduction of natural gas for cooking, while coal remained the primary fuel source for residential heating through the early 1920s. Automatic mechanical coal furnace stockers had extended the life of coal for heating, but by 1927, more than four million homes had switched over to natural gas and oil for heating. The most popular heating source for homes that continued for a long time was oil burner boilers to heat water, which heated the house using steam radiators. By the late 1920s, 66% of homes had electricity, which allowed General Electric to introduce thermostats and automatic blower fans to enable residents to regulate their heat from furnaces, introducing central forced-air heating.

George believed that there was opportunity and growth in the heating and stove industry. He was also interested in innovation and considered himself an amateur engineer. George worked in the heating and stove industry for his entire career. Beginning his career with the Calvert Stove and Heating Company, he held positions as a stenographer,[144] book-keeper,[145] salesman,[146] and vice president.[147] By 1934, he operated his own company in Baltimore as both a direct-to-consumer and a wholesale distributor for the Sheppard and Caloric Stove Companies.

Marge and George Bartolomeo, circa 1928

While George worked in the stove business, he met his future wife, Marjorie Decker. They met while Marjorie was a receptionist at the gas company and George was getting his start in the gas stove business, having most recently joined the Calvert Stove Company. George married Marjorie Heilman Decker on August 27, 1927, at St. Bernard Church Rectory.[148] Marjorie was not a member of the Catholic Church at the time, so she received a special disposition from the Church (Mixtum Matrimonium) to marry George. The marriage sacrament was witnessed by George's brother and sister, Albert and Florence Bartolomeo, and officiated by Father Joseph Hauck.

Marjorie grew up in Baltimore at 108 North Baltimore Street, born to Conrad and Nannie Heilman. Marjorie's father, Conrad, worked as a day laborer.[149] By 1916, her parents were separated. Her mother later married Clement Decker and lived at 211 Walnut Avenue.[150] Clement worked as a salesman for the local gas company. By 1930, Clement Decker was the proprietor of his grocery store[151] and learned the butchering business, which benefited the family in future years, as WWII brought an era of consumer product shortages and food rationing in 1941.

Dick, Marjorie, Joe, George, circa 1940

George and Marge bought their first home at 1333 Gorsuch Avenue[152] circa 1928. The home was a 1,300-square-foot brick row home in the

Waverly/Coldstream section of North Baltimore with a covered porch in the front of the house. Homes in the neighborhood were arranged with an alley and chain-link fence separating the backyards. In the 1920s, residential dial-tone phone service revolutionized communications for families, making it easy to stay in touch. George and Marge had their first "home phone number," **CHE**sapeake 2955, only 32 years after Giovanni had arrived at Ellis Island.

George and Marge's first child, George Joseph Bartolomeo Jr., known as Joe, was born on August 16, 1930.[153] Their second son, John Richard (Dick), was born on December 3, 1937.

Their home was located across the street from Baltimore City College's new campus and the newly expanded Baltimore Municipal Stadium, a popular location for growing families.

George was an avid football fan who closely followed football and regularly attended Loyola High School games. George attended football games almost weekly, going to Memorial Stadium or watching city league games at Clifton Park with his son Richard. Memorial Stadium was the center of sports activity for all Baltimoreans. The Baltimore Municipal Stadium hosted the Baltimore Orioles from 1944, and the Baltimore Colts also made the stadium their home in 1947. Many of Baltimore's biggest city rivalry games took place at Memorial Stadium. Two of the biggest games played every Thanksgiving Day were City vs. Poly, and Loyola vs. Calvert Hall. Other local rivalries included The University of Maryland Terrapins versus Johns Hopkins, and the Navy

Midshipmen vs. Army or Notre Dame.

George and Marjorie were two very different personalities, and their relationship as a couple was very complementary. George was known as quiet, civil, and generous to everyone. A lean man, he dressed smartly in a classic dark brown fedora, a Bulova wristwatch with a brown leather band, and well-cared for brown leather shoes, with his hair always neatly cropped and his face clean-shaven. George enjoyed playing the violin and was primarily self-taught. He had a creative mind, a strong work ethic, and enthusiasm for new ideas and inventing new devices. One of his early inventions was converting an old beer bottle case into a grass catcher on the back of his push lawnmower so that he did not need to rake the grass clippings after cutting his lawn.

While George was always contemplating new ideas and his next project, Marjorie took action. She had a lot of energy, providing commentary and insight on everything and everyone. Marge was energetic in every way, ready for whatever the day brought. An avid reader, she consumed multiple fiction and non-fiction books weekly. She undoubtedly possessed Baltimore's most worn library card, always recommending new books to others. Marjorie rarely sat still except to read, constantly starting new projects and not stopping until they were completed.

OUR AMBITION
"FOR MEN ONLY – THE 8 O'CLOCK MASS ON THE SECOND SUNDAY"

ST. BERNARD'S HOLY NAME

NEWS

VOL. 4 FEBRUARY 1947 NO. 2

GEO. BARTOLOMEO ELECTED PRESIDENT OF HOLY NAME SOCIETY

At the last regular meeting, held on Monday, January 13th, the following were elected officers for 1947:

Geo. Bartolomeo - Pres.
Martin Dippold - V-Pres.
Wm. Gallagher - Secy.
John S. Clarke - Treas.
Dave Barry - Marshal

George Bartolomeo has been a member of our parish for many years, and is known, admired and respected by all for his hard work, especially in the junior activities of the parish. He has served as Treasurer for two terms, and for the past two years has been Vice-President. His intimate knowledge of the needs of the Society, his reputation

MONTHLY MEETING

A MESSAGE FROM
OUR PRESIDENT

Dear Men:
At the last meeting of the Holy Name Society I was honored by being elected president of your organization. This is, indeed, a high honor, and I am deeply grateful for this consideration. I fully realize that with honor goes a measurable amount of responsibility. I accept these responsibilities, and assure you that during the time I am in office I will use my best efforts to promote the welfare

George Bartolomeo Elected President of Holy Name Society

Both George and Marge were proficient gin rummy players; in the evenings, after a long day on the water or at the beach, both enjoyed a game of gin rummy together. George had fine-tuned his card skills playing weekly games with a rotation of priests in the Baltimore Diocese.[154]

George and Marge were involved in many social activities and led organizational programs for their family's church and children's high schools. George was elected president of the St. Bernard's Holy Name Society in February, 1947. He had previously served as the vice president and treasurer for two years.[155] George and Marge were members of the Sodality of the Blessed Virgin, participating in charitable work for the diocese. Marjorie was active in the Loyola High School Mother's club and the Women's Civic League Gardening Committee. She was also an avid bowler competing in the local women's duckpin league.

Marjorie Bartolomeo

Regarding a Baltimore gardening contest of which Marjorie was a judge, *The Evening Sun* reported on July 30, 1963, that "*Mrs. George Bartolomeo, covering the Hamilton Area, commented: A few outstanding gardens, but many need better care. Some have beautiful plant material, but they are too crowded. People seem to be carried away with a desire for quality and quantity without thought of overall design or appearance.*"

Marge was 84 years old and still going full steam ahead in her life. Once, when she visited her grandson at his home in California, Marge had decided that the previous homeowners had planted roses on the wrong side of the house based on the ability to receive adequate sunlight. She proceeded to remove all of the rose bushes and replant them. George and Marjorie were also very active and diligent with their physical activities. They walked around the 30-acre Clifton Park reservoir almost daily and were avid swimmers. When Marge vacationed at the beach with grandchildren, friends would look on in amazement as the 84-year-old leaped up, ran into the ocean waves, and proceeded to swim up and down the coast.

The house on Gorsuch Avenue was their home until the family moved to 3603 Woodlea Avenue sometime before 1956.[156]

ALBERT BARTOLOMEO

Albert Bartolomeo, circa 1936

Loretta and Albert Bartolomeo, 1965

Albert, the youngest of the boys, often referred to as "Babe," began work as a clerk at the Baltimore Enameling Company in 1920.[157] In 1923 he was working at the Jones Hollow Ware Company, first as a bookkeeper,[158] and then in 1930[xxxv] as a traffic manager.[159] The Hollow Ware Company manufactured cast iron stove ware and door stops inside the Baltimore Penitentiary using prison labor, employing 240 convicts at 75 cents per day.[160] After 1914, a wave of prison reform took hold in the U.S., prompting the Maryland Department of Corrections to reconsider the use of convict labor for private business. By 1915, the Maryland Correction Board had begun reviewing contracts and programs using penal labor for outside companies, and by 1918 the prison was no longer accepting new contracts. By the end of the 1920s the state had transitioned prison labor for the exclusive use of state roadwork. While working with the prison representing the Jones Hollow Ware Company, Albert met Loretta McNamara, his future bride, who worked at the Baltimore Correctional Institution.[161] On June 26, 1928, *The Baltimore Sun* newspaper reported, *"Romance In Penitentiary Due To Reach Climax Tomorrow – A.L. Bartolomeo, civilian stenographer, and miss Loretta McNamara, office employe[sic] at Institution, to be married in St. John's Church."*

Loretta grew up on 809 Eager Street across the street from the Baltimore Correctional Institution, and her father was a Baltimore police officer.[162] Albert and Loretta were married on June 27, 1928, at St. John

xxxv In the 1930 Federal Census, Albert stated that he did not attend high school. He most likely attended Thomas Johnson Public School based on the location of the family's residence in Baltimore.

Catholic Church located at Eager and Valley Streets, with the Reverend John J. Dillon officiating.[163] Albert and Loretta resided at 4908 Arabia Avenue.[164] In 1941, Albert registered for the draft and listed his position as a salesman for McCardle and Walsh, a commercial heating and plumbing supply company.[165] In 1956, Albert took a new position as a salesman for American Pipe and Equipment.[166]

Albert with Knights of Columbus "Cheese Club" plaque, 1971

Loretta, Thomas, Albert Bartolomeo, 1960

Albert and Loretta had four children—Albert Joseph, born October 11, 1933; John Patrick, on June 10, 1936; Mary Loretta, born June 14, 1937; and Thomas Lawrence, born November 25, 1940. Albert and Loretta were lifelong members of St. Dominic Catholic Church on Harford Road in the Hamilton neighborhood of Baltimore. All four children attended school at St. Dominic. Albert was very active in his community and St. Dominic Church. He was a member of the Knights of Columbus, The Order of Alhambra, Alcala Caravan, and a charter member of the "Cheese Club." The Cheese Club was aptly named since the Catholic Church designates Friday as a day of penance, and Catholics never ate meat on a Friday. The men from the Knights of Columbus met every Friday night for card games, donating the winnings to a local charity[167]or struggling parish.

The Knights of Columbus Council was founded in 1887, officially receiving its charter in 1910 as Baltimore K of C, Council #205, located on Harford Road in the Hamilton section of Baltimore.

In 1924, Archbishop Michael Curley dedicated the Knights of Columbus Alcazar Ballroom, located on Cathedral Street, where the Councils held special events. In 1970, Albert was honored by the Knights of Columbus during a formal ball held at the Alcazar, recognizing him as the oldest surviving charter member of the Knights of Columbus's Baltimore Council #205.

Albert and Loretta enjoyed weekend retreats, and rail service from Baltimore provided easy access to Manhattan. The B&O Railway operated the Royal Blue rail service between Baltimore and New York City. Travel by train, particularly on the Royal Blue, was a pleasant experience offering premier services on the B&O's Royal Saxony Blue cars. The passenger car's exterior was accented with gold leaf trim, and the interior, which was entirely crafted in mahogany, consisted of comfortable, enclosed vestibules where the passengers sat. While Albert and Loretta enjoyed Broadway shows and everything Manhattan had to offer, the four children remained behind with "Mrs. Helen," the babysitter. Mayhem often ensued but would return to normal on Albert and Loretta's return to Baltimore.

Albert and Loretta adored their grandchildren and spent most Sundays with them. As the family expanded, the dining table grew with them. The Sunday dinner special was usually McNamara's Irish Spaghetti, an Irish interpretation of meatballs and pasta using chunks of ground beef and cans of sauce. The Irish and Italian influences in the home provided a lot of love and entertainment. If St. Patrick's Day fell on a Sunday, the children received a special treat as Albert paid his homage to Loretta's "McNamara heritage." Albert would slowly pour the children's milk into their glasses. The milk would turn green as the white liquid was poured into the clear cup, astonishing the kids. The children always enjoyed their time with their grandparents.

Albert and his family lived on Arabia Avenue in Baltimore their entire lives. The brick duplex home had a large, covered porch where the family sat on summer evenings to greet neighbors passing by on the sidewalk. The cement steps led up to the home's front door. The front door opened into the living room, which had a welcoming fireplace with a picture above the mantle. Draped across the frame would be palm fronds from last season's Palm Sunday Mass. Proceeding through the dining room to the kitchen, one would come to a back door that led to the fenced-in yard with its single-car garage, which always housed a new shiny Plymouth.

The fireplace and elegant dining room table were exceptionally festive during the Christmas season.

Christmas Midnight Mass was a mainstay, since Albert's two sons, Buck and Jake, were altar boys serving at Midnight Mass. After Midnight Mass, the family would return home at 2 a.m. and quickly retire in anticipation of Christmas and Loretta's big Christmas breakfast.

Christmas was a day of shuttling between the relatives, stopping by to see George and Marge, and then spending the afternoon with Anna and Gus Pfeifer.

Albert Bartolomeo, 1931

Arundel Boat Club members' pin

Thomas Bartolomeo, Albert's youngest son, fondly recalled his early memories of his father at the Arundel Boat Club located south of the Baltimore Harbor. Currently, it is the location of Johns Hopkins Bayview.

"I have the pin he wore as a member of the Arundel Boat Club. Albert and his brother George were in the boat club and rowed four- or eight-man sculls. I remember them throwing the coxswain of the winning boat crew into the water. They also had canoes and paddled to Betterton and Tolchester, tied their canoes together, and slept in them. Not sure if they were married or if their wives went along. When Albert, George, Louis, and Gus (August Pfeifer) got together at our house, they played a card game called 'Pitch.' I have one picture of Dad playing golf at Clifton Park in Baltimore. I remember Dad telling me, "You can fool some of the people some of the time, but you can't fool all of the people all of the time."

Albert lived a life of service to his church and philanthropic organizations. He was benevolent and supported charities that helped those who were less fortunate. Hardworking and diligent, he committed Sundays and holidays to his family. Entertaining his grandchildren with magic and providing blithesome days for their enjoyment gave Albert great joy.

Albert passed away on March 2, 1972, and Loretta on September 12, 1972. Both were interred at Most Holy Redeemer Cemetery.

FLORENCE BARTOLOMEO YANNI

Florence Bartolomeo Yanni

The family's youngest member, Florence, received her confirmation sacrament at St. Mary, Star of the Sea Church on May 25, 1919. She lived in Baltimore at 2763 Fenwick Avenue with Giovanni and Rose until 1930, when she was 22.[168]

In 1929, after the stock market crash and at the start of the Depression, women were making gains in employment and professional careers.

Florence had become successful in her professional career and prospered. She may have been one of the first businesswomen in the 1920s to own a car.

The Baltimore Sun newspaper reported that on December 11, 1929, "*Florence A. Bartolomeo's car was stolen from Fenwick Avenue and returned the same day by Baltimore Patrolman Fred Kahler.*"[169]

In the 1930 Federal Census, Florence stated that she was working as a stenographer for a medical company. In the 1940 Federal Census, she reported that she had completed four years of high school. Florence most likely attended St. Joseph's School of Industry,[xxxvi] located several blocks from the Fenwick Avenue residence. She graduated around 1925/1926. St Joseph's, which became Seton High School in 1926, offered a business curriculum for girls, which was consistent with Florence's employment.

On Monday, April 6, 1931, Florence married Louis Yanni. They were married in Baltimore, and Reverend Leo J. McCormick performed the ceremony.[170] The records do not state the church's name, but it was most likely St. Francis of Assisi. In 1931, Reverend Leo J. McCormick was a priest at St. Francis of Assisi; there are no marriage records for St. Francis of Assisi before 1940. He also served at St. Dominic Catholic Church, and there was no church record of Florence and Louis's marriage at St. Dominic Church either. Reverend Leo J. McCormick served many locations in the Baltimore Diocese, later becoming the assistant head of the diocese school system.

---

xxxvi Education records were not located for Florence.

Louis Yanni

Florence and Louis Yanni resided at Louis's home at 866 Broadway in Bayonne, New Jersey. Florence was Louis's second wife; Louis was previously married on April 23, 1923, to his first wife, Eleanora Petrone. Louis and Eleanora were married for five years when Eleanora passed away at the age of 24 on July 23, 1928, in their home at 866 Broadway, Bayonne, New Jersey.[171] The 1930 U.S. Federal Census identified Louis as a 31-year-old widower.

Louis immigrated to the U.S. via Ellis Island in 1916. For 50 years, from 1925 until 1975, Louis was a barber and the proprietor of the O.K. Barbershop located in Bayonne, New Jersey. Previously, Louis lived with his sister Virginia Yanni and her husband Spiro Gargano in Jersey City.

Florence is listed in the 1940 Federal Census[172] as living with Louis and as the proprietor of a retail ladies' clothing store in Bayonne, N.J. The 1950 census lists Florence as holding the position of stenographer. Florence and Louis resided with Louis's mother, Angelina, and Louis's son from his first marriage, Raymond, age 16, and their son Louis Jr., who was eight. Based on the age of their son Raymond (16) as listed in the 1940 census, and since Florence was still living on Fenwick Avenue in Baltimore ten years prior in 1930, Raymond was Louis's son from his first marriage.

Louis's U.S. WWII draft registration lists him as a barber, born in Torre de' Passeri, Italy, on November 30, 1899, the same village in Italy from which the di Bartolomeo family had immigrated in 1893. The Yannis were close friends of Giovanni and Rosaria's. Giuseppe's (George) di Bartolomeo's baptismal certificate dated May 7, 1899,[173] from The Church of the Holy Rosary in Jersey City states that Giuseppe (George) di Bartolomeo's godfather was Giuseppe Yanni. The Yannis must have been very close friends of Giovanni for Giuseppe Yanni to become their son's godfather.

—— CHAPTER ELEVEN ——

1929

The Great Depression

"The migrant people, scuttling for work, scrabbling to live."

—— **John Steinbeck**

Closing Baltimore Stocks—Late Wall Street Prices

5 ★★★★★ Wall Street Markets

THE EVENING SUN

5 ★★★★★ Wall Street Markets

STOCK CRASH HALTS, PRICES REBOUND

SALES TOTAL MORE THAN 12,880,000

HOPE OF SAVING 52 MEN ON LAKE VESSEL FADES

Good Evening

LOBBY PROBERS FAIL TO NETTLE PENNSYLVANIAN

ITALIAN PRINCE FIRED UPON IN BELGIAN CAPITAL

REPORT DITEMAN PLANE IS FOUND IN SEA IS DENIED

BANKERS' REASSURANCES CHECK WILDEST SELLING IN YEARS AFTER BIG DROPS

Many Issues Topple $10 To $40 To New Lows For Year As Market Is Totally Demoralized—Ticker Hours Behind

REPLIES TO MARGIN CALLS NOT AWAITED BY BROKERS AS ACCOUNTS ARE WEAKENED

Baltimore, front page news, October 24, 1929 stock market crash

On Thursday, October 24, 1929, Wall Street experienced panic selling, which was the start of the Great Depression in the United States. Interest rates were increasing, commodity prices for farm goods were dropping, tariffs were expanding, and Americans lost confidence in the American economy. The drop in Wall Street stock prices created financial losses for shareholders of company stock. The losses were accelerated when people bought stocks on margin and then rushed to sell their stocks to minimize their losses, which continued to accelerate the decline of share prices. By the time the Depression hit rock bottom in 1932, the economy had contracted by 85%, 50% of home mortgages were in default, one-third of the banks in the U.S. had failed and closed their doors, unemployment was at 25%, and for those who had jobs, their incomes had dropped by 40%. In addition to cities being devastated by the financial losses, the southwest region of the United States was experiencing a severe drought. Sharecroppers were being pushed off farms for not paying the landowners. The multi-year drought began a historical migration of southwestern farmers out of Oklahoma, who took on the three-day journey on Route 66 to California. These events caused one of the most significant cultural transitions in American history as Americans became more reliant on government programs.

In 1933, President Franklin Roosevelt launched the National Industrial Recovery Act and the Social Security Administration. Progressives introduced unemployment relief programs to establish a minimum wage, 40-hour workweek, bank reform, and repeal of prohibition. Roosevelt also established programs that created meaningful jobs to get people back to work through the Works Progress Administration (WPA), which launched work programs for infrastructure projects. The WPA program started a new era of industrialization in America that included building airports, roads, bridges, dams, and schools. To begin improving the lives of rural populations, Roosevelt launched the Rural Electrification

Administration and the TVA to bring electricity to rural Americans. One of the most extensive New Deal programs created that benefited workers in Baltimore was building new communities to combat homelessness and provide affordable housing for Americans. The government developed three master-planned communities under the government's New Deal. They were Greenhill, Ohio, Greendale, Wisconsin, and Greenbelt, Maryland. Greenbelt, Maryland, located 30 miles outside of Baltimore, employed thousands of workers building roads, sidewalks, schools, apartments, row homes, parks, and bridges. The WPA also launched additional projects around the city that included the construction of Pretty Boy Dam, Herring Run Reservoir, Savage River Bridge, and Patapsco State Park, all helping to get Baltimore back to work.

After the economy hit rock bottom in 1932, the recovery was slow. Still, six years later, in 1938, Franklin Roosevelt's New Deal programs began an era of progressive reforms and allowed the Democratic Party to dominate politics for 28 years and maintain control of the White House, except during the Eisenhower administration. Dwight Eisenhower's popularity as the Supreme Allied Commander in World War II, combined with recurring concerns over Korea and the "communist threat" gave Eisenhower a landslide win, taking 55% of the popular vote to beat his opponent Adlai Stevenson.

Although Baltimore experienced a severe downturn during the Depression, the Baltimore economy did not suffer to the same degree as other major cities. Baltimore's diverse economy experienced a lower unemployment rate than other major cities, such as New York and Chicago, where major financial institutions played a more prominent role in the city's economy. The impact of the Depression was less damaging to the non-durable goods, food, and clothing sectors of the economy.

Financial institution failures had a significant impact on families in America. The largest bank failure was The New York-based Bank of the United States, with $200 million in deposits. Locally in Baltimore, Chesapeake Bank and Baltimore Trust Company both failed. Baltimore-based Westheimer Investment Company did not survive the Depression, and all employees lost their jobs. August Pfeifer, who was employed by Westheimer Investment Bank, worked his way up to bookkeeper[174] for Mr. Westheimer. The Westheimer family was prominent in the Baltimore business community. Ruth Gutman Westheimer's family were German immigrants who founded Gutman's Department Store in Baltimore. Their son, Julius Westheimer, became a national financial advisor, partnering with Louis Rukeyser on the television program *Wall Street Week.*

During the Great Depression, family members supported each other with whatever was required to make it through any financial challenges impacting them. By 1930, August Pfeifer had taken a new position in the life insurance business[175] with Peoples Life Insurance Company. Giovanni, always the conservative, had spread his savings account deposits across several banks. When banks closed and failed to remain solvent, several banks offered him discounted residential properties in lieu of cash, which they could no longer return to their depositors. During the worst period of the Depression, Giovanni acquired five homes at distressed prices and became a profitable landlord.

The Bartolomeo families were able to sustain their standard of living during the Depression. Additionally, they survived the downturn because the families had not taken on debt and were financially conservative. None of the family members lost their homes, and they continued to thrive.

Attention Builders
GAS RANGES
Pipe and Pipeless Furnaces
FOR IMMEDIATE DELIVERY
SHEPPARD STOVE COMPANY
Eastern Ave. & Chester
Wo. 3214

Baltimore Sun newspaper advertisement for Sheppard Stove Company

In 1934, during the Depression, the parent company of George Bartolomeo's stove, gas and heating business suffered financial problems. However, George continued to invest in his business. He expanded his operations in the mid-Atlantic region by acquiring the interest of all principals in the stove company who had not survived the economic decline. On May 23, 1934, *The Baltimore Sun* reported, "*Sheppard Stove Company, Incorporators, Charles S. Austin Sr. George J. Bartolomeo and Arthur W. Baker, Authorized capital stock, 100 shares, no par value.*"

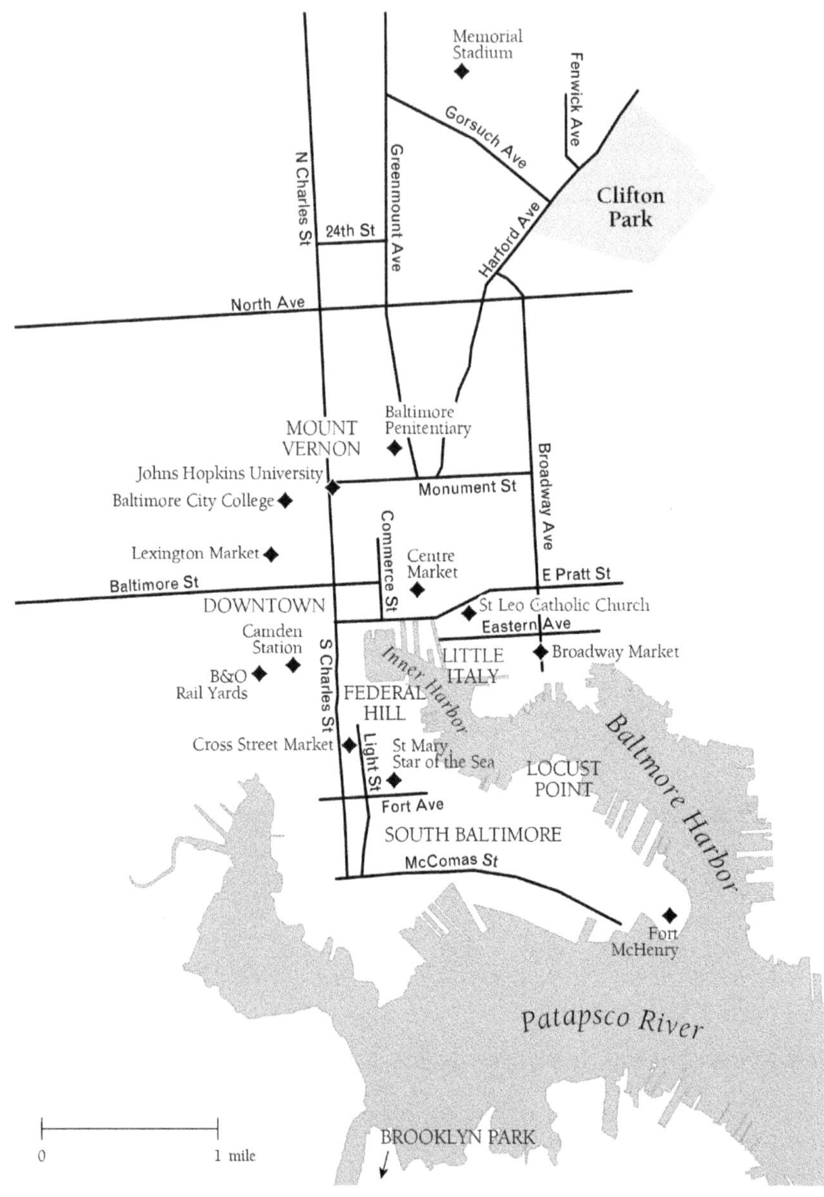

Map of Baltimore, location of Family residences and points of interest, circa 1906.

— CHAPTER TWELVE —

1932-1937

Giovanni Considers Retirement

"Every day the increasing weight of years admonishes me more and more that the shade of retirement is as necessary to me as it will be welcome."

— **George Washington**

By 1928, Giovanni and Rosaria's children had moved from South Charles Street and were prospering as the heads of their own families. As Maria, Casper, Louis, Anna, George, Albert, and Florence all left home and started their families, Giovanni and Rosaria decided to make their last move, relocating from renting 1501 South Charles Street and purchasing a comfortable home at 2763 Fenwick Avenue.[176] This location was in an area known as the Alameda/Coldspring area and was across the street from Clifton Park. The home was a two-story row house with a covered front porch and a second-floor bay window.

For the first time, Giovanni considered stepping away from his shoe business. The craft that had supported and built his family over the past 38 years was in decline. While his children prospered in new companies (electronics, stove, steel manufacturing, and carpentry), his prospects were fading. Having started their journey 38 years ago, settling in Brooklyn, Jersey City, and Baltimore, he repeatedly saw that the shoemaking business was transforming and accelerating its mass production of factory-made shoes. There was no longer a need for bespoke craftsmanship, as new shoe stores like Edison Brothers and Stern Bauer were opening everywhere, providing inexpensive shoes. They were even making the soles of shoes from rubber. *"Il mondo sta volgendo al termine!"*[xxxvii] Automation in the shoe business hastened with the invention of the "Goodyear Welt," which uses a machine for gluing a thicker rubber sole onto the bottom of a shoe. The process had been available for several years, but the industry remained fragmented. In the early 1900s, the shoe manufacturing industry began to consolidate. The United Shoe Machinery Company formed a conglomerate by acquiring McCay Lasting Machine Company, Goodyear Shoe Machinery Company, Epper Wely Company, and Davey Pegging Company. The time it took to attach a sole to a shoe was reduced from 20 minutes to 20 seconds, and the price was six times cheaper than when handsewn. The consolidation of the shoe manufacturing industry brought efficiencies and allowed for the broader distribution of finished goods. By 1912, the U.S. Shoe Machinery Company had a monopoly in the shoe-manufacturing industry, and in 1945 they were indicted under the Sherman Anti-Trust Act.

---

xxxvii The world was coming to an end.

Even though automation had taken over the process of attaching the sole to the leather uppers, there was still an opportunity for shoemakers to make a good living. Since the shoes' uppers still needed sewing by hand, many shoemakers, including Giovanni, contracted with shoe companies to tan, cut, and sew the shoe, then send the completed upper shoe to the manufacturer, who attached the sole and inventoried the finished product. By 1918, employment in the shoe-manufacturing industry was rapidly growing, and the compensation gap widened. In 1918, 2,000 shoemakers were making shoes as sole proprietors, earning $25 per week, which was 44% higher than a factory shoe worker earning $17 per week.[177]

By the late 1920s, production methods improved, gaining efficiencies and providing more options to the consumer. The demand for bespoke shoes and contract work was in decline. The artisan's ability to work the leather, talent to create a perfect fit, on-the-job apprenticeship, and working as a journeyman shoemaker was no longer required.

The industrialization in America, its remarkable ability to innovate, and demand for a large working class were what had led Giovanni to come to America. Now the outlook for his family's prospects was more dynamic than ever, and at the same time, thousands of years of shoemaking knowledge was being cast away and forgotten, the craft obsolete. Giovanni's work was coming to an end, but not yet.

Rosaria spent her later years with the grandchildren, for whom she cared greatly. The next generation provided Rosaria with 16 grandchildren. She always carried a box of licorice hidden deep in the pockets of her heavily pleated skirt and provided the children candies whenever they were together.[178] The Good 'n Plenty candies reminded her of her home and the licorice flavors from the Menozzi De Rosa candies she was familiar with as a child in Torre de' Passeri, where the area is one of the largest cultivators of the licorice extract plant, Glycyrrhiza.

— CHAPTER THIRTEEN —

1950

George and Marge Bartolomeo Move to Woodlea Avenue

George Bartolomeo playing violin

George and Marge's new home on Woodlea Avenue was a detached brick house with a large screened-in front porch. In front of the house was a perfectly manicured Kentucky Blue Grass lawn separated precisely down the middle by three concrete steps that led to a short sidewalk to the home's screened front porch. The porch had an iron slider sofa with floral plastic cushions, perfect for viewing activities on the front street and greeting neighbors who were out for a walk along the sidewalk.

When entering the house, to the right, there was a fireplace with a Seth Thomas clock on the mantle, which took three keys to wind and chimed on the quarter-hour in the living room. The dining room was on the left side of the staircase, and the living room was on the right. A staircase that led up to the house's second floor split the two rooms. Upstairs were three bedrooms and a bathroom tiled with small black and white tiles. The kitchen was in the back of the house, with a rear door that led to an immaculately maintained backyard. The gardens featured a cement birdbath recessed into the ground and framed by perfectly pruned rose bushes and gladiolas. The kitchen had a Formica-top table with chrome legs, and a black rotary phone always sat on the table. The stove and refrigerator were white, and the Frigidaire had a rounded freezer at the top.[179]

When the family members would arrive for Sunday dinner, George often played opera music on the record player. He would confidently attempt to accompany the opera with his violin, playing along with the recorded music. When his grandchildren arrived, George would perform magic tricks, making coins come out of their ears then making the quarters disappear. Next, he would make a rabbit out of a white handkerchief that he always carried in his left breast pocket before making the handkerchief rabbit jump up the length of his arm. After finishing his music and magic show, he would take the grandchildren down to the basement. The underground level, with its single window to let daylight in, was a special place for George and his grandchildren to explore. That's where George's workshop was. He enjoyed playing the role of curator, orienting the grandchildren about the latest gadgets he had invented and items that no longer had any use, like his gas mask from when he was the block warden for air raid drills during WWII. The children were permitted to rummage through Joe's Marine Corps. footlocker, examining medals, hats, and jackets. Also stored in the basement were bottles of wine. George would always pour the grandchildren either a drop of wine or vermouth into small glasses.[180]

Marge and George often hosted their families for Easter and Thanksgiving dinners. In addition to attending Mass, Easter Sunday also involved an Easter egg hunt, using colorful plastic eggs that contained pennies, and "egg tapping" competitions. The firewood pile in the backyard, stacked with split logs for the fireplace, was always a target for hiding the coin-filled plastic eggs. The rules of engagement for the Easter egg hunt were simple. The grandparents would hand everyone a straw-colored wicker Easter basket, and the grandchildren would forage for the plastic eggs that the grandparents had hidden before the children arrived. As a small child standing at the starting line with a wicker basket, the area that needed to be covered would have seemed larger than the grounds of Windsor Castle. The front and backyards would erupt in a mad rush as siblings and cousins searched for purple, yellow, blue, pink, and red eggs. Green eggs were the most difficult to discover, and the grandparents always looked confused at the end when the number of eggs returned did not match the number of eggs hidden. Legend has it that there are still green plastic eggs hiding in the green lawns of Baltimore.

After an afternoon of Easter festivities, it would be time for dinner. Marge would serve either a fresh pork roast or sour beef and dumplings. If it was Easter, fresh pork roast with the outer skin scored into tiny squares was on the menu. While the pork was sitting on the kitchen table before being joined by its vegetables and escorted to the dining room, George would join the grandchildren to pick off the pork skin (cracklings) and enjoy the crunchy, fat-soaked delicacy. By the time the roast would make its way to the dining room table, it would be battle scarred and sufficiently picked at by George and his grandchildren, but it was always tasty and served with mashed potatoes and peas with lots of butter.

After dinner, the grandchildren would be dismissed, and they'd take a 15-minute walk up Woodlea Avenue's quiet, tree-lined street to Walther Avenue, being careful not to stumble on the broken sidewalk misshaped by 100-year-old tree roots. Then they would enjoy a snowball at the Walther Gardens snowball stand. The plywood structure housed a server behind a window, who shaved the ice and asked for your selection or flavor. The "Skylight Blue" flavored syrup was always a favorite, and if the grandchildren had the extra pennies, they would order soft marshmallow goo on top. The blue syrup mixed with melted marshmallows and ice was a treat on summer nights. The walk back to the house would give them just enough time to crunch the last sweet, gooey crystals before the water from the melting ice would wholly collapse the paper cones.

Walther Gardens Snowball Stand, founded 1933

George and Marge stayed active throughout their lives. They took many beach vacations with their extended family and traveled to visit their grandchildren in other parts of the country. They were proud of their family, enjoyed spending time with George's brothers, and were always available to help anyone needing assistance.

George passed away in 1983 at the age of 84,[181] and Marge in 1999 at 94.[182]

CHAPTER FOURTEEN

Family Recreation and Leisure

"And along the shores of these varied waters rose land of the most inviting nature: At times broad fields, at other times gently rising land covered with trees even taller than those on the island, and everywhere the impression of opulence, and quietness, and gentle living. It was the most congenial place he had ever seen.

One thing he was certain: Along this splendid river he wished to spend the rest of his life."

— James Michener, Chesapeake

As young couples in the 1920s, the families enjoyed active social lives, staying close to brothers and sisters and adding new friends. Most recreational activities centered around the Chesapeake Bay and its estuaries on both the western and eastern shores of the northern part of the bay. Couples and family members, mainly George's brother Albert and wife Loretta, regularly got together for boat outings and competitions at the Arundel

Marjorie Bartolomeo, circa 1925

Boat Club. They used canoes rigged with a simple mainsail or paddled their canoes across the Chesapeake Bay. A frequent destination was Tolchester Beach. Tolchester Beach was a popular beach resort destination where couples went for the day to see amusements, picnic on the beach, and watch horse racing. Located on Maryland's Eastern Shore, the resort was reached by taking a two-hour boat ride from Light Street at the Baltimore harbor to Tolchester on the "Louise," a side-wheel steamship. The Louise was a grand, double-deck 232-foot boat, with music and entertainment on the upper deck.[183] Betterton Beach was another popular destination for George, Marge, Albert, and Loretta. Located on the Chesapeake Bay's Eastern Shore, it was a two-and-a-half-hour boat ride, providing another way for Baltimoreans to escape the city's summertime heat. Like the "Louise" that transported people to Tolchester, Betterton Beach visitors used the "Bay Belle," a 206-foot steamship. The resort was in the northern section of the Chesapeake Bay, on the Sassafras River. Betterton, Maryland, was initially founded as a convenient location for shipping produce from the Eastern Shore. Its ideal location near the Chesapeake and Delaware Canal provided easy access for its locally grown produce to be transported to Delaware and New Jersey.

Albert and George Bartolomeo, circa 1925

Sidewheel Steamer Louise

Interest and attendance at Eastern Shore resort towns declined when the Chesapeake Bay Bridge was built and opened in 1952, giving automobile access to the Maryland ocean beach resort of Ocean City, Maryland. The 4.3-mile steel suspension bridge officially opened for travelers on July 30, 1952. The bridge's commemoration on opening day was a momentous event and included all-day festivities at Sandy Point State Park. The ease of access soon positioned Ocean City, Maryland, as the number one resort destination for families driving from Baltimore. Growing up, many of Giovanni's great-grandchildren spent their summers enjoying the sandy beaches and body surfing the crashing waves of Ocean City, Maryland. The Betterton and Tolchester resorts eventually closed in 1962 as other locations for alternative vacations became more easily accessible.

Louis, John, and the family dog enjoying a day on the river, circa 1923

Louis and Julia enjoyed weekends and summers with family and friends at Orchard Beach. The "shore house" was the center of activities for the extended family when brothers, cousins, and grandchildren came to spend the weekend. Louis's sons, John, Roy, and Earl, enjoyed fishing, crabbing, and spending time on the water with their father. Going fishing with their father is where they learned the value of getting up early, patience, the power of mother nature, and "keep your line in the water."

In 1935, George and Marge rented a second home on the Magothy River for the summers. The Magothy River, located an easy 30-minute commute from downtown Baltimore, was a picturesque river that flowed 2.5 miles upstream from the Chesapeake Bay. The river was accessed from Baltimore Lighthouse with Sandy Point on the south side and Gibson

Island at the north entrance. George and Marge stayed at the same cottage every summer, located on the widest point of the Magothy River. In the summer, Joe and Dick lived at the shore from the day school let out until the dreaded return to school in the fall. The two-bedroom clapboard cottage with its screened porch, where Joe slept, was one of 12 homes that shared a community shower. The cedar shake bungalows were modest, but for a 12-year-old boy, there wasn't anything better than sleeping on a wood-framed canvas cot with the moonlight on the bay as a night light and the gentle hum of a small Evinrude two-stroke echoing against the tree-lined shore as an alarm clock. The experience of living on the river every summer were lifelong memories for all family members. During most days, Joe worked as a lifeguard at the nearby beach, MagoVista. On Saturday mornings, Pop Decker and Dick would go fishing and crabbing. The weekends were always busy with guests, and on Saturday afternoons, Albert, Loretta, and their family would go to the cottage to spend the day. Sundays, the only day that the boys wore shoes, they'd go to the church in Severna Park and stop by Dawson's, the local general store, for provisions and "picked-while-you-wait" tomatoes and corn from the local farm stand. While at the Magothy, their son Joe and Charles Austin, the son of George's business partner, enjoyed crabbing and fishing with cane poles fitted with woven green lines and red-and-white wooden bobbers for flounder, perch, and striped bass (rock fish). There were occasional days when they would luck into a large school of fish, furiously pulling the

Charles Austin and Joe Bartolomeo, circa 1938

double hook rigged cane poles out of the water. The fishing was so good that when the hook, baited with either a minnow or blood worm, went under, it would hook two fish at a time. There were days when they returned to shore with the boat filled to the gunnels with fresh fish. The boys would have to sit cross-legged on the transom and bow to make room for their bounty.

George Bartolomeo (center), Clement Decker (right)

Dick and Joe kept crab traps and slough boxes and had dozens of Maryland blue crabs on hand at all times. The overwhelming number of crabs they caught and maintained in live boxes allowed them to share their catch with neighbors, and Marge to spend hours at the kitchen table picking crabs for crab soup and crab cakes. Crab feasts with the neighbors and family were held on weekends, when others would join them after completing their workweek in Baltimore. There was always a refrigerator full of soft crabs waiting for the frying pan and a bushel of hard shells ready to be steamed. With the abundance of crabs, there was always a large crab pot on the boil.

Retrieving newly sloughed soft crabs for crab sandwiches was a highlight of the summer. Maryland blue crabs shed their shells several times a year, and almost immediately, the shell body begins to harden. To get the best soft-shell crabs, people at the shore kept slough boxes. As soon as a crab backed out of its shell, it would be removed from the slough box and prepared for eating. First, the cook would use scissors to cut across the top of the soft shell, peel it back and remove the lungs and gills, then flip over and peel back the pointed tab on the bottom and remove. Cooking the crab was simple: Lightly flour and sauté in a pan, five minutes each side, place between two pieces of bread with a just-picked, big fat slice of sweet Maryland Eastern Shore tomato, add salt and pepper, and enjoy the crunchy, salty, sweet soft-crab sandwich.

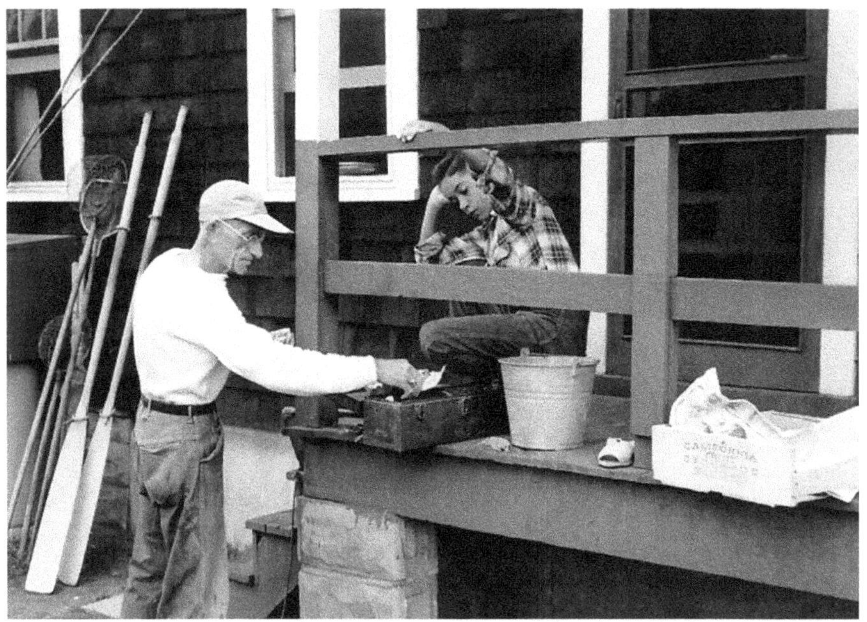

Pop Decker, (Marge's father) and Dick Bartolomeo, getting ready to catch Saturday night's dinner, circa 1951

Spending summers on the estuaries of the Chesapeake Bay, Joe learned how to be a world-class oyster patter. Beginning the recipe with six dozen oysters to feed six people, Joe would shuck the fresh oysters. Only about 90% of them would make it to the patted oyster process, since Joe would eat many of them immediately after shucking, enjoying the cold, clean, salty, mineral flavor of freshly harvested oysters.

Joe would start the recipe using locally harvested Chesapeake Bay Eastern Shore or Chincoteague oysters, rolling them in a cracker meal, salt, and pepper mixture. Selecting two oysters, he would place the two oysters slightly overlapping, the fat plump belly of one oyster against the flat section of another. He would gently pat them together in cupped hands and then lay them in a dish. Once the oysters had completed their first pat-down, they were placed in the refrigerator for two hours to "bleed," the processes of letting the patted oysters lose some of their juices. After two hours, Joe would start the whole patting process again for the second round of fine cracker-meal patting. He would gently lay the oysters in a pan with grease and butter, letting them sizzle in the hot oil, turning after two minutes, and then moving them to a paper plate. He would finally transfer the fried oysters to the dinner plates and serve them with horseradish sauce, red potatoes, coleslaw, and Maryland Eastern Shore corn on the cob.

In his 1940 memoir *Happy Days*, H.L. Mencken described the Chesapeake Bay of his youth as an *"immense protein factory"* out of which Marylanders *"ate divinely."*

At the end of an active summer day on the water, everyone would have had their fill of crabs, corn on the cob, and tomatoes. The sunset would stretch down the river, creating a sheet of sparkling diamonds broken by tiny ripples from a single rowboat returning to the dock. The evening would end with playing cards with friends from the neighboring cottage.

The two constants in the lives of Louis and Julia, George and Marge, and Albert and Loretta were spending time with family, friends, and relatives enjoying summer retreats at the shore, and social events at their church.

— CHAPTER FIFTEEN —

January 15, 1937

"Giovanni's Last Shoe"

"Shoes are symbolic of the past, present, and future paths that we walk, and a good shoemaker protects you from the hardships of the journey."

— **G. Mark Bartolomeo**

On January 15, Giovanni woke up in their house on Fenwick Avenue. He could immediately tell from the absence of any ambient sound that snow had fallen during the night, creating a sound barrier that absorbed any noise from outside. Giovanni listened to the silence, a solitary figure in his shop's early morning gray light, quiet now that the house had not awakened to start its day.

The new year was underway, and Giovanni had several orders to complete for clients looking forward to wearing the latest shoe styles. There were new shoes for children, serious business shoes for people in business, work boots for men to start their new jobs, and trendy, fashionable shoes for women to wear for the new spring season.

When Giovanni handled a shoe, even with his callous hands, he could sense the shoe's purpose by its weight, the soles' thickness, and the texture of the leather upper. Even the smell of the leather would give away something of its purpose: the tanning proteins used for work boots differed from those Giovanni used for the highly polished modern-day oxfords. Moving his hand down the side of the shoe's uppers and feeling the broguing, each shoe made a different sound from one shoe to the next. Every pair was unique, just like his customers. Fifty-nine years of making shoes had taught the shoemaker and father of seven that people were different from one another; none were better or worse, just like the shoes he made. Every shoe, like every person, was created to do a specific job. The shoes he made for workers with solid stitching, thick soles, and reinforced toes were just as important as the shoes he made for young ladies with delicate stitching and light, flexible soles for dancing—just like the ideal person, the ideal shoe needed to fit the job.

As Giovanni started his work for the day, the silence in the home was pierced by the soft pinging of his last hammer on the hand-carved wooden last. In a single fluid motion, he wrapped the leather upper smoothly around the last, his contorted fingers pulling the leather taut while his swollen palm smoothed the wrinkles in the toe of the shoe. He instinctively reached for his trimming knife; its wooden handle worn from years of use. He sensed the familiar, comforting fit in his right hand, trimmed the excess edges of the leather, and looked to his left for the stiff leather sole that he then affixed to the bottom of the shoe.

As he advanced in age, Giovanni often thought back to his life in

Torre de' Passeri and the decision that he and Rosaria had made 34 years ago to bring their family to America. As difficult as the decision had been, he knew that all journeys are the bridge from who we are to what we can become. Life had changed forever once he boarded the ship in Naples. Making the easy choice of staying in Abruzzo and not taking the journey would have been sure to leave them with few experiences and no opportunities for his sons and daughters. Leaving while his family was still young had kept them all together. If they had not departed at that time, he was confident that his sons would have made the journey independently as they grew older and weary of life in Italy. By making the journey together, the family encountered few hardships in America. His children had found their place, creating the lives they wanted and succeeding in their chosen work while starting their own families. Just like the shoes he built, Giovanni recognized the differences in his children and how each had chosen their path.

The shoe he now held in his hand was a calf-high, lace-up boot with a low heel, built to comfort the wearer during long days of standing. As he pulled the waxed cord through the shoe's leather, he felt the heat of the cord and smelled the beeswax melting into the shoe's recess and sealing the hole. The calf-high shoe was the style of boot that his oldest daughter, Maria, preferred. He was proud of Maria's decision to commit her life to the service of others and her selfless commitment to those that were less fortunate. Maria's family was the largest of all his children's—The Sisters of St. Francis. They had all chosen a life of humility. Maria's future was secured with a family bonded together that endured hardship and poverty through contemplation and service.

Using a punch and awl to brogue the next shoe for one of his customers, Giovanni noted that this shoe was intended for traveling while also providing the wearer with the added feature of brogue uppers. This shoe was the most popular style of the day in America, seen on the feet of almost everyone that passed on the street. It reminded him of his son Gaspare, who he and Rosaria had named after one of the three wise men who had brought gifts to the desert, diligently searching for something special in the wilderness beyond their kingdoms. Similarly, Gaspare continued his journey beyond the di Bartolomeo family's destination to find a life, unlike Giovanni had imagined. Gaspare had a vision and dream that was different from the others in the family. He must have imagined a bigger, better life beyond where the family had settled in Baltimore and decided to continue his own journey. Giovanni respected Gaspare's decision to create a new life and make so many changes, and Gaspare seemed to be comfortable with being "less Italian" than his family. He had succeeded in starting a new company, serving his country during the World War, and building his own family.

Giovanni shifted on the workbench, turning several small rolls of waxed cord on their side while trying to find a more comfortable position. At 79 years old, sitting at the workbench caused his shoulders to stiffen and knees to ache. The cramping of muscles across his lower back from bending over the bench, soreness in the thumb joint from pulling the leather across the last, and squinting to see the fine handiwork of the leather exhausted him. Releasing a long breath, he considered the many years since he had started the journey from Torre de' Passeri with his five friends. He was 35 at the time and had already mastered his shoemaking craft. Leaving the village that day, Giovanni couldn't have imagined what they were going to experience in the future. The six men who had made the journey together were confident of their abilities and content with their decision, knowing that they could provide for their families once they arrived in America. Traveling together had offered an opportunity for each of the men to discuss and refine their plans. Of the men, Giovanni was the closest to Francesco Favicoli and Giuseppe Forna, both builders. Francesco was a skilled carpenter who built many of the structures and furnishings in Torre de' Passeri. Giovanni admired the work and skill of people who used raw materials and then shaped them into something of beauty and purpose. Giovanni's son Luigi reminded him of Francesco. Both had great talent and the confidence needed to combine detailed plans with natural materials and make something incredible. Men like Luigi were good at solving problems because they had the patience to plan and the vision to create something new. Luigi had not only been a skillful carpenter but had also built a great life with a wonderful family and many friends.

Giovanni did not notice it earlier, but the morning sun's rays had already reached through the front window, and the reflection of the light from the snow illuminated the far corner of the front room. In the corner of the room sat a player piano used to entertain the family. Twenty-two years ago, the family had brought the piano home to their Fort Avenue home.[184] Whenever he thought about the piano, he could hear its resonant tones from long ago. He reached for the next shoe; a T-Strap shoe made for dancing that one of his customers needed for an upcoming event. The delicate stitching and flexible sole made the wearer light on their feet, and the well-made uppers gave the dancer support. Celebrations were always a highlight in the di Bartolomeo household. Anna often had her friends over to the house, and they would dance as they played music on the player piano. Anna's kind spirit brought joy and happiness to everyone. She loved to dance, listen to music on the radio, attend movies, and explore the city with her friends. As the first of Giovanni's children to be born in America, Anna had enthusiastically adopted the American lifestyle. She was forward-looking, optimistic about the future, and generous. Anna's way of thinking was different than her father's. He was born in a rural village, with limited exposure outside of his community, while Anna was his first to grow up in a modern, lively metropolitan city and had been a teenager during the vigorous growth of Baltimore, experiencing everything that the city had to offer.

The home was awaking with the aroma of freshly brewed coffee, the sound of Rosaria's footsteps, and the light clink of utensils in the kitchen. Giovanni set aside the T-Strap shoes and rose from the bench to take a break. He walked over to the steel percolator on the white porcelain counter in the kitchen. The transparent glass knob on top of the pot showed brown liquid circulating through the coffee maker. Grabbing the ceramic handle on the side of the chrome vessel, Giovanni poured a short cup of Eight O'Clock coffee as the steam from the hot liquid condensed on the thick, smooth round edges of the white mug. Rosaria was already busying herself with baking anise pizzelle and citrus almond cookies in preparation for a visit from the grandchildren that afternoon. Rosaria enjoyed the noisy visits and the children's excitement for her licorice candies and fresh-baked anise cookies.

The sweet, medicinal, earthy caramel of the anise combined with the bittersweet vanilla of the almonds were reminders of Giovanni's childhood when his mother, Annantonio, would bake cookies for the family. Grabbing an almond cookie with his coffee, he anticipated the pleasant sensation of the still-warm cookie melting in his mouth, combining the flavors of almonds, lemon, and sugar.

Back to the front of their home and onto his stained and scarred workbench, he reached for his wooden last and a new piece of leather for his next shoe. He was working on several pairs of shoes in various stages of completion, and he felt an uneasy urgency to finish for some unknown reason. The anxious feeling of time compressing had been with him all day.

He knew the next shoe well. Giovanni had worked with the owner of the shoe for many years. It was a no-nonsense, plain brown oxford with no broguing or gimping, a cap toe, and waxed leather laces that belonged to a professor at the local college. What else should a professor wear? The oxford shoe, named after Oxford University, was the most appropriate shoe for a professor to wear. The oxford shoe fits the job; if you attended college, you must wear oxford shoes.

Giovanni always enjoyed speaking with the professor, who was well-versed in many subjects, maintained an earnest, pleasant tone, and had a curious, mischievous look as if he knew something but did not want to share. Giovanni and the professor would talk about the economy, which in 1937 was beginning to recover from the Great Depression. The professor reminded Giovanni of his son Giuseppe—inquisitive, perceptive, knowledgeable on many subjects, and always amicable with strangers, friends, and families. Giuseppe, too, had enthusiastically pursued education as a student at Baltimore City College, where he had been the first of the children to complete fours year of high school.[185] Giovanni had thought that Giuseppe should be a professor with all of this education. But Giuseppe had seen opportunities during his early days working at the Calvert Stove Company and had decided to stay in the stove business after completing high school and start his stove and heating company. Giuseppe had also recently started a family and lived nearby on Clifton Park.

Giovanni finished off the oxford shoe with a brilliant shine and a cap toe, adding a slight touch of refinement.

Winter's mid-afternoon sunlight was already dimming and wouldn't last much longer, and Giovanni needed to complete work on two other shoes. He picked up one of the latest styles of men's shoes, the spectator.

This shoe was to be two-tone with full brogue tops and low heels. This shoe was the ideal shoe for an outdoor sporting gentleman. It had a casual, comfortable design to be worn by someone who wanted to be well dressed and comfortable while at sporting events.

Alberto had become an avid sportsman and had taken up golf, boating, and rowing the eight-man scull at the Arundel Boat Club.[186] Family and friends all called him "Babe" since, at the time, he was the youngest in the family. Another Baltimorean and great sportsman, Babe Ruth, also wore the "spectator" shoe style. Alberto enjoyed getting together with his friends and family and spending time at Clifton Park and Mount Pleasant Golf Courses, which had recently opened just down the street from Fenwick Avenue. Alberto and his wife Loretta were doing well, and their family continued to grow. Giovanni smiled while thinking about how active Alberto and his family had become at St. Dominic Church.

The short winter's day was coming to an end. Through the house's front window, the shoemaker noticed the street lamps' lights reflecting off the snow, and still, there was one last shoe to complete. The new style was called a pump. It had a swirl strap across the front that fastened around the ankle, and a thin sole with two-inch Cuban heels. Giovanni had not seen many shoes of this style. The shoe was popular with "career women" who had office jobs. This shoe required a little extra attention, since its leather straps were delicate, and Giovanni had difficulty getting it right. The person who wanted the work done was a stenographer at the local hospital. The shoe owner reminded Giovanni of his daughter Florentina, who had also been a stenographer and had recently opened her own dress shop. Her women's fashion shop was prospering, as was Louis's barbershop. Giovanni was content knowing that his son-in-law Louis, the son of an old family friend also from Torre de' Passeri, was doing so well.

As he was retired, Giovanni had not intended to spend the whole day at the repair bench. Having worked with so many people in Baltimore over 33 years, the shoemaker still enjoyed keeping up with his favorite customers, learning about their views on politics, the latest developments in Baltimore, and the news of their families. As a close friend to many customers, he always looked forward to hearing about their different types of work and the stories of their family gatherings.

The light of day was gone, he felt time compressing and Giovanni's Waltham pocket watch read 5:10 p.m.[187]

Giovanni and Rosaria resided at the Fenwick Avenue home until Giovanni's passing on January 15, 1937 and Rosaria's in 1938.[188]

"ON this wondrous sea,
Sailing silently,
Knowest thou the shore
Ho! Pilot, Ho!
Where no breakers roar,
Where the storm is o'er?"

—— ***Emily Dickenson***

Epilogue

"We all come from the past, and children ought to know what it was that went into their making, to know that life is a braided cord of humanity ...."

—— **Russell Baker**

Letter From Joe Bartolomeo to his Brother Dick Bartolomeo[xxxviii]

Dear Dick,

I felt that the future ahead of us could be short (not like Mom and Grandma Decker[xxxix]*) and not much to dream for; however, I realize that every day is a gift from God, filled with challenges, joys, hopes, and dreams.*

I realize that to our siblings, we never do grow old. In our minds, we are still the kids that fished, crabbed, and swam at Magothy Villa for those many years, went to Orchard Beach in the summer to visit the Brooklyn Barts, rode the Transit bus to Loyola High School and College, ate mom's crab cakes, steamed crabs with Mom and Pop Decker.

And all the years of Easter egg hunts in the backyard on Woodlea Ave. Sadly we have been separated for many years, but the bond of brotherhood is never broken. These memories will last over time and space.

One of the saddest things is that our children never had the chance to grow up near each other, but when they are together, it is like they have never been apart. I know that Mom and Dad would be proud of the wonderful men and women we have raised. All have the strong ethic of Dad and the moral integrity of Mom.

They would also marvel at their great-grandchildren, as I do every day with pride at how they turned out.

Joe

xxxviii On November 11, 2009, at the age of 79, Joe Bartolomeo wrote a letter to his younger brother Dick Bartolomeo, who was attending a church retreat. Joe shares with Dick his thoughts on growing old and family bonds.

xxxix "Grandma" (Marge) lived to age 94, Grandma Decker, her mother, lived to age 101.

During the 14th and 15th centuries, the Medicis' launched the Renaissance period of Italy with the belief that art and societal achievements are done in the search for perfection and pride, not financial reward. Artisans passionately dedicated to their craft were ultimately rewarded for their extraordinary talent, art, and craftsmanship. However, the more significant benefit was the personal satisfaction of doing your craft well. By relentlessly pursuing perfection, monetary rewards followed.

Twentieth-century shoemakers from Italy, Ferragamo, Bontoni, and Mecdariello were all admired for the quality and unique style of their shoes. Still, Giovanni also built a fine family, showing them the way and protecting them from the journey's hardships.

As the last of Giovanni's children and their spouses passed away, family history disappeared with them. Close family friends helped and comforted the family along the way, but their names and stories are lost. Now that the first generation is gone, additional details about their personal lives will never be known. Over several generations, we lose understanding of our ancestral journey, holiday traditions, family secrets, and the common knowledge of the past that bonds families.

Giovanni left Italy for better opportunities in America, knowing that he was responsible for the welfare of his family. His journey was not to provide better opportunities for himself, but to ensure a better outcome in life for his children and future generations. And his progeny did start their own journeys, pursuing opportunities that built better futures for themselves and their families.

Afterword

While writing this book, it became apparent that, in those years, families spent their time very differently than we do today. Extended family members gathered for holidays regardless of distance or circumstances, weekend recreational activities were family-oriented, and the Catholic Church played a central role in their lives. Leisure time was much more valued, and, as adults, the bond of sibling relationships continued to form the core of their social lives.

This book's description of Giovanni and Rosaria's lives was constructed from personal stories contributed by family members and genealogical data collected since 1999. Ensuring that personal and authoritative information about their lives and immigration experiences survive for future generations was the overall motivation for writing this book.

In addition to providing detailed accounts of Giovanni and Rosaria's lives, an underlying objective was to make the book enjoyable while also providing readers with the historical context.

As the story evolved and indicated the need for more detail, additional information was acquired through independent researchers, archivists, parish employees, and genealogists located in Italy, New Jersey, and Baltimore. The research done in Italy provided copies of the original artifact and source citations of marriages, births, deaths, and legal proceedings in the di Bartolomeo family between 1690 and 1897. Organizations were contacted directly for missing information, including The Church of Santa Maria delle Grazie in Torre de' Passeri, the Catholic diocese of Baltimore, The Sisters of St. Francis Convent, Baltimore City College, the New Jersey public school system, the New Jersey Historical Society, Virginia Office of Vital Records, Library of Congress, the Social Security Administration, The Church of the Holy Rosary, the City of Baltimore Health Department, Maryland State Archives, cemeteries, newspaper archives, and high schools. In-person interviews and site visits were also used for information gathering. They included interviews with residents of South Charles Street in Baltimore, Maryland Archives, Virginia Archives, Cross Street Market, and The Church of the Holy Rosary in Jersey City, New Jersey. Access to government documents provided reliable citations and sources of details to document family residences, marriages, military service, business directories, immigration, and other facts relevant to establishing the framework for The Giovanni and Rosaria di Bartolomeo Family Historical Narrative.

Immigration records were accurate with minimal errors, names accurately documented, personal details of passengers effectively transcribed with further information of the passenger's origins and destination. Information on the di Bartolomeo family varies, some "life event" details are available for some children, and that same information is missing for others.

Some genealogical data remains unknown, or supporting documents are unavailable. Over time, many schools, businesses, and churches have closed forever. For example, churches that had large parishes are now closed. In Baltimore, the family's church, St. Mary, Star of the Sea, merged with Baltimore's Holy Cross Parish, joining Our Lady of Good Counsel parish and consolidating into the Catholic Community School of South Baltimore, which has since closed its doors in 2009.

The exact date of the di Bartolomeo family's relocation from Jersey City to Baltimore is unknown but did occur in the six-month timeframe between June 1905 and January 1906. Since no school records were available showing when the children began school in Baltimore, we can only use Federal Census data for Jersey City and Baltimore and the self-reported information recorded in the census reports to narrow the timeframe.

Specific incidents that may have prompted Casper to create a new identity for himself and his family are unknown. Casper changed his name to Casper B. Lawrence, changed his place of birth from Italy to Jersey City, New Jersey, and renamed his parents, John D. Lawrence and Rosana L. Bartholomew, on his application for his social security account number. He, again, recorded his place of birth as Jersey City, New Jersey, in the 1930 Federal Census and 1940 Federal Census for West Virginia.

During the writing of this book, *Giovanni's Last Shoe*, every effort was made to provide only known information supported by official source citations. The events that do not have supporting documentation are identified as such. Any approximate dates and methodologies used to narrow down the timing of events are identified as estimates and the source referenced.

Acknowledgments

Many family members shared stories about their ancestors and provided personal insights to make Giovanni and Rosaria's journey more engaging for the reader. The additional records collected were supported by many people,[xl] including Joe Bartolomeo and Carolyn S. Bartolomeo, who maintained their collection of family photographs and personal effects of George (Giuseppe) over the past 60 years. Dick Bartolomeo, the youngest son of George (Giuseppe) Bartolomeo, provided personal stories about his father George and his maternal grandfather Pop Decker. Dick's early family memories, and the personal letter from his brother Joe reinforces the bond of family across time and space. Dick's memories of summers spent on the Magothy River give a glimpse into an idyllic world of nature, recreation, and family time. Thanks to Dick's input into the content of this book, we were able to revisit the value of multi-generational relationships that many grandchildren cannot experience in today's mobile society.

Thomas Bartolomeo, the son of Albert ("Babe") and Donna Bartolomeo, Albert's daughter-in-law, provided information and

xl Attempts were made to reach extended family members and ancestors of Giovanni and Rosaria. Several were unable to respond.

understanding of important family holiday events and how the church played a critical role in their family. *Giovanni's Last Shoe* benefitted from Tom and Donna providing photographs of Albert and Loretta Bartolomeo and memories of Albert's involvement in his community supporting underprivileged youth. Additionally, Donna provided proof reading of the early manuscript. Mary Bartolomeo Oppelt, Albert's only daughter, provided photos and long-forgotten stories about Albert and a family dedicated to helping their community. Mary's forethought in 1984 to create and save a recorded interview of Anna Bartolomeo Pfeifer provided details not available anywhere else.

Anna Bartolomeo, Louis's granddaughter, provided narratives regarding Louis's life at "The Shore," reinforcing how families spent their leisure time together. Anna was the primary contact between Louis Bartolomeo's family members in Baltimore, Maryland, and me. Her collection of photographs and solicitation of cousins, brothers, and sisters provided memories from the ancestors of Louis Bartolomeo. Anna graciously shared the details of her grandfather's life.

Deborah Pfeifer Morrissey represented her siblings, providing information and detailed accounts of the lives of her grandparents, Anna and August Pfeifer. Anna's story benefited from Deborah's time to outline family holidays and memorable events she and her sister Bonnie shared with Anna on their road trip to Atlantic City. Deborah also shared a 1982 recorded interview that she made with Anna.

Original artwork and creative cover designs were developed by Jinjer

Markley. The "About the Author", was written by Jordan B. Layson. Maps depicting Giovanni's journey were custom designed by cartographer, Nat Case, INCase LLC.

Many thanks for the feedback from the manuscript's beta readers, John Campbell and Simon Burden. Photo restoration was by Duc N.

About the Author

Giuseppe (George) Bartolomeo, Mark Bartolomeo, circa 1976

Mark Bartolomeo is a great-grandson of Giovanni and Rosaria di Bartolomeo, the main characters in the book, and grandson of George (Giuseppe) Bartolomeo. Mark spent more than 20 years working with researchers and genealogists in Italy, New Jersey, Maryland, and Virginia, sourcing and organizing information for his first non-fiction book, *Giovanni's Last Shoe*. He is a native of Baltimore growing up where the di Bartolomeo family settled, and a graduate of the University of Maryland.

In retirement, Mark and his wife Lee reside in Florida, where he competes in triathlons and Washington, DC, on Capitol Hill, where they spend time with their granddaughter.

You can contact the author or follow *Giovanni's Last Shoe* below.

Contact details;

email - giovannislastshoe@gmail.com

APPENDIX

di Bartolomeo Family Timeline

YEAR	DATE	NAME/EVENT	LOCATION	NOTES
1696	N/A	Ferdinando di Bartolomeo Born	Torre de' Passeri	Giovanni Paternal Great-Great-Great-Grandfather
N/A	N/A	Lucrezia Cappalletti Born	Torre de' Passeri	Giovanni Paternal Great-Great-Great-Grandmother
1739	N/A	Giosafatto di Bartolomeo Born	Torre de' Passeri	Giovanni Paternal Great-Great-Grandfather
1746	N/A	Nicola di Nicolantonio Born	Torre de' Passeri	Rosaria Maternal Great-Great-Great-Grandmother
1750	N/A	Generosa Domenico Born	Torre de' Passeri	Giovanni Maternal Great-Great-Grandmother
N/A	N/A	Filippo Santoro Born	Torre de' Passeri	Giovanni Maternal Great-Great-Grandfather
1750	N/A	Pasquale di Lorenzo Born	Torre de' Passeri	Rosaria Paternal Great-Great-Grandfather
1752	N/A	Antonia Cappola Born	Pescara, Abruzzo	Rosaria Paternal Great-Great-Grandmother
1757	N/A	Anna di Tullio Born	Torre de' Passeri	Giovanni Paternal Great-Great-Grandmother
1760	N/A	Giovanna di Tullio Born	Torre de' Passeri	Rosaria Maternal Great-Great-Great-Grandmother
1773	N/A	Ferdinando di Bartolomeo Died	Torre de' Passeri	Giovanni Paternal Great-Great-Great-Grandfather
N/A	N/A	Lucrezia Cappalletti Dies	Torre de' Passeri	Giovanni Paternal Great-Great-Great-Grandmother

1774	N/A	Gustino di Lorenzo Born	Pescara, Abruzzo	Rosaria Paternal-Great-Grandfather
1774	N/A	Lucia Nicoli Born	Pescara, Abruzzo	Rosaria Paternal Great-Grandmother
1776	4-Jul	The United States of America Declares Independence	Philadelphia, PA.	U.S. War for Independence 1775–1783
1777	N/A	Nicola di Proserzio Born	Torre de' Passeri	Giovanni Paternal Grandmother
1778	N/A	Paolo di Bartolomeo Born	Torre de' Passeri	Giovanni Paternal Grandfather
1787	N/A	Giuseppe di Nicolantonio Born	Torre de' Passeri	Rosaria Maternal Great-Great-Grandfather
1788	N/A	Domenica Martino Born	Torre de' Passeri	Rosaria Maternal Great-Great-Grandmother
1789	29-Aug	Giovanni Santoro Born	Torre de' Passeri	Giovanni Maternal Grandfather
1795	24-Sep	Domenica Rocco Born	Moscufu, Pescara	Giovanni Maternal Grandmother
1796	N/A	Nicola di Nicolantonio Dies	Torre de' Passeri	Rosaria Maternal Great-Great-Great-Grandmother
1802	N/A	Dionora di Nicolantonio Born	Pescara, Abruzzo	Rosaria Paternal Grandmother
1806	17-Jun	Raffaele di Lorenzo Born	Pescara, Abruzzo	Rosaria Paternal Grandfather
1808	N/A	Filippo Santoro Dies	Torre de' Passeri	Giovanni Maternal Great-Great-Grandfather
1811	N/A	Giosafatto Bartolomeo Died	Pescara, Abruzzo	Giovanni Paternal Great-Great Grandfather
1811	N/A	Anna di Tullio Died	Pescara, Abruzzo	Giovanni Paternal Great-Grandmother
1811	N/A	Francesca Varrasso Born	Abruzzo	Rosaria Maternal Grandmother

1812	27-Aug	Gustino di Lorenzo Died	Pescara, Abruzzo	Rosaria Paternal Great-Great-Great-grandfather
1814	10-May	Napoleonic Rule of Italy Ends	Italy	Italy Divided Austria/Sardinia/Sicily
1817	N/A	Camillo di Nicolantonio Born	Abruzzo	Rosaria Maternal Grandfather
1817	N/A	Giovanna di Tullio Died	Torre de' Passeri	Rosaria Maternal Great-Great-Great-Grandmother
1818	20-May	Antonia Cappola Died	Abruzzo	Rosaria Paternal Great-Great-Grandmother
1819	N/A	Paolo di Bartolomeo/ Nicolo Proserzio Married	Torre de' Passeri	Giovanni Paternal Grandparents
1821	11-Feb	Giosaffatte Antonio di Bartolomeo Born	Torre de' Passeri	Giovanni Father
1822	23-Dec	Annantonio Santoro Born	Torre de' Passeri	Giovanni Mother
1826	N/A	Generosa Domenico Died	Torre de' Passeri	Giovanni Maternal Great-Great-Grandmother
1828	N/A	Anna di Tullio Died	Torre de' Passeri	Giovanni Paternal Great-Great-Grandmother
1832	25-Feb	Raffaele di Lorenzo/ Dionora Marriage	Pescara, Abruzzo	Rosaria Paternal Grandparents
1837	6-Nov	Angelo di Lorenzo Born	Abruzzo	Rosaria Father
1840	21-Sep	Nicola di Proserzio Died	Torre de' Passeri	Giovanni Paternal Grandmother
1841	5-Aug	Giosaffatte di Bartolomeo Married Anna Santoro	Torre de' Passeri	Giovanni Parents
1841	25-Oct	Anna Domenica Carmela Born	Torre de' Passeri	Giovanni Maternal Grandmother
1842	5-Aug	Annantonio Santoro Married Paolo di Bartolomeo	Torre de' Passeri	Giovanni Great-Grandparents

1844	12-Nov	Camillo di Nicolantonio Married Francesco Varrasso	Torre de' Passeri	Rosaria Maternal Grandparents
1845	20-Aug	Giovanni Santoro Died	Torre de' Passeri	Giovanni Maternal Grandfather
1845	31-Oct	Filomena di Nicolantonio Born	Abruzzo	Rosaria Mother
1847	1-Dec	Paolo di Bartolomeo Died	Torre de' Passeri	Giovanni Paternal Grandfather
1858	24-Jun	Giovanni Born	Torre de' Passeri	Son of Giosaffatte Antonio di Bartolomeo
1858	20-Oct	Lucia Nicolai Died	Pescara, Abruzzo	Rosaria Paternal Great-Grandmother
1862	N/A	Giuseppe di Nicolantonio Died	Torre de' Passeri	Rosaria Maternal Great-Great-Grandfather
N/A	N/A	Domenica Martino Died	Torre de' Passeri	Rosaria Maternal Great-Great-Grandmother
1863	3-Jul	Battle of Gettysburg	Gettysburg, PA.	Gen. George Meade and Robert E. Lee
1865	9-Apr	American Civil War Ends	Appomattox, VA.	Acceleration of Industry and Railroads
1865	12-Nov	Camillo do Nicolantonio Died	Torre de' Passeri	Rosaria Maternal Grandfather
1865	20-Dec	Angelo di Lorenzo Married Filomena di Nicolantonio	Torre de' Passeri	Rosaria Parents
1866	1-Jan	Unification of Italy	Italy	Capture of Venice from Prussia
1867	6-Nov	Rosaria Born	Torre de' Passeri	Daughter of Angelo di Lorenzo
1871	19-Aug	Giosaffatte Antonio di Bartolomeo Died	Torre de' Passeri	Giovanni Father
1873	17-May	Dionora di Nicolantonio Died	Pescara, Abruzzo	Rosaria Paternal Grandmother

1880	5-Apr	Raffaele di Lorenzo Died	Pescara, Abruzzo	Rosaria Grandfather
1885	3-Jan	Lorenzo Varrasso Died	Abruzzo	Rosaria Maternal Grandfather
1886	1-Dec	Northern Italy Begins Industrialization	Milan, Italy	Fiat Launches in Turin, 1899
1888	15-Sep	Giovanni Married Rosaria	Torre de' Passeri	Santa Maria delle Grazie
1888	27-Sep	Annantonio Santoro Died	Torre de' Passeri	Giovanni Mother
1889	1-Dec	Maria di Bartolomeo Born	Torre de' Passeri	a.k.a. Sister M. Siegberta
1892	7-Jul	Gaspare di Bartolomeo Born	Torre de' Passeri	a.k.a. Casper Bartholomew Lawrence
1893	21-Aug	Giovanni Immigration to Ellis Island	Naples to Ellis Isl.	Steamship Cachemire
1893	25-Aug	New York City Hurricane	New York	Category 1, 85 mph
1893	18-Oct	Move to 509 Baltic St., Brooklyn, NY	Brooklyn	Giovanni's first US residence
1893	18-Oct	Giovanni Immigration Petition	Brooklyn	Living at 509 Baltic St., Brooklyn, NY
1894	29-Mar	Luigi di Bartolomeo Born	Torre de' Passeri	a.k.a. Louis Bartolomeo
1895	2-Jun	Resided at 157 1/2 Jackson Ave.	Jersey City, NJ	di Bartolomeo family first US residence
1896	23-Sep	Julia Rowland Born	Baltimore	Wife of Louis Bartolomeo
1897	12-Jan	Rosaria, Maria, Gaspare, Luigi Immigration to Ellis Is.	Ellis Island	Steamship Werra
1897	2-Dec	Anna di Bartolomeo Born	Jersey City, NJ	a.k.a. Anna Bartolomeo Pfeifer
1898	25-Jun	August Pfeifer Born	Baltimore	Husband of Anna Bartolomeo

1899	22-Feb	Giuseppe di Bartolomeo Born	Jersey City, NJ	a.k.a. George Joseph Bartolomeo
1899	N/A	Tony Verrosso Married Filomena di Nicolantonio	Del./Wash., DC	Marriage of second husband
1899	30-Nov	Louis Yanni Born	Torre de' Passeri	Husband of Florence Bartolomeo
1900	20-Feb	Loretta McNamara Born	Baltimore	Wife of Albert Bartolomeo
1900	20-Oct	Alberto di Bartolomeo Born	Jersey City, NJ	a.k.a. Albert Bartolomeo
1903	17-Dec	Wright Bros First Flight	Kitty Hawk, NC	Wilbur trains pilots at Univ. of Md. 1917
1904	28-Feb	Francesco Varrasso Dies	Teramo	Rosaria Grandmother
1905	9-Jun	Resided at 54 Harrison Ave.	Jersey City, NJ	U.S Federal Census, NJ, 1905
1905	26-Jul	Marjorie Heilman Decker Born	Baltimore	Wife of George Bartolomeo
1906	8-Jan	1301 Eastern Ave. (residence listed by Giovanni)	Baltimore	Giovanni Declaration of Intent
1908	5-Oct	Florentina di Bartolomeo Born	Baltimore	a.k.a. Florence Bartolomeo Yanni
1910	21-Apr	Resided at W. McComas St. Baltimore	Sparrows Point	1910 U.S. Federal Census
1910	23-Aug	Maria Enters Convent as Sister M. Siegberta	Philadelphia	Sister of St. Francis
1912	15-May	Titanic Sank	North Atlantic	1,157 Lives Lost of 2,208 Onboard
1915	13-Jun	Louis Bartolomeo Marries Julia Rowland	Baltimore	St. Mary, Star of the Sea
1916	20-Jan	Resided at Fort Ave. and Light St.	Baltimore	Reported in Baltimore Sun Jan. 20, 1916

1917	6-Apr	World War I	Global	Military infrastructure developed
1917	5-Jun	Louis Bartolomeo Registers for WWI	Baltimore	Working at Bartlett-Heyward
1917	11-Oct	Casper Lawrence Enters WWI	Camp Meade	Communications Morse Code Instructor
1918	20-May	George Graduates Baltimore City College	Baltimore	The year is accurate; the day is estimated
1918	12-Sep	George Bartolomeo Registers for Draft WWI	Baltimore	Employed at Sheppard Stove Co.
1919	9-Apr	Anna Bartolomeo Marries August Pfeifer	Alexandria, VA	Alexandria, VA marriage certificate
1920	13-Jan	Giovanni resides at 1501 S. Charles St. Baltimore	Baltimore	1920 U.S. Federal Census
1920	17-Jan	Prohibition	1920–1933	Illegal MFG, Sale and Transport of Alcohol
1923	3-Jul	Casper Lawrence Marries Cecelia Bradbury	Wheeling, WV	St. Joseph's Cathedral
1927	27-Aug	George Bartolomeo Marries Marjorie Decker	Baltimore	St. Bernard's Rectory
1928	27-Jun	Albert Bartolomeo Marries Loretta McNamara	Baltimore	St. John Catholic Church Baltimore
1928	28-Dec	Tony Verrosso Died, Filo. di Nicolantonio 2nd husband	Washington, DC	Arlington National Cemetery
1929	29-Oct	Great Depression	United States	Collapse 1929–1933; Recovery 1934–1936
1929	29-Oct	Black Tuesday Stock Market Crash	Wall Street	85% of economic value lost
1930	5-Apr	Resided at 2753 Fenwick Ave.	Baltimore	Giovanni Retires
1930	21-Sep	Filomena di Nicolantonio Died	Washington, DC	Arlington National Cemetery

1931	6-Apr	Florence Bartolomeo Marries Louis Yanni	Baltimore	Baltimore, MD marriage certificate
1937	15-Jan	Giovanni Bartolomeo Died	Baltimore	Most Holy Redeemer Cemetery
1938	5-Nov	Rosaria Bartolomeo Died	Baltimore	Most Holy Redeemer Cemetery
1940	22-Jul	Julia Rowland Bartolomeo Died	Brooklyn Park, MD	Holy Cross Cemetery
1941	7-Dec	Pearl Harbor Attack	Pearl-Oahu, Hawaii	2,403 Lives Lost, 1,178 Injured
1942	25-Apr	Louis Bartolomeo Registers for WWII	Baltimore	Working at Wm. C. Scherer
1945	6-Aug	Atomic Bombing of Hiroshima and Nagasaki	Japan	Approx. 200,000 Lives Lost
1945	10-Sep	Louis Bartolomeo Naturalization	Baltimore	U.S. Naturalization Records
1946	14-Jan	Maria Sister M. Siegberta Naturalized	Havre de Grace, MD	Sisters of St. Francis
1952	25-May	August Pfeifer Died	Baltimore	Most Holy Redeemer Cemetery
1954	3-Jul	Maria Died (Sister Mary Siegberta)	Havre de Grace, MD	Calvary Cemetery Conshohocken, PA
1960	31-Jul	Louis Bartolomeo Died	Brooklyn Park, MD	Holy Cross Cemetery
1969	16-Jul	Apollo 11 Moon Landing	Earth's Moon	Launched from Cape Canaveral
1972	2-Mar	Albert (Alberto) Bartolomeo Died	Baltimore	Most Holy Redeemer Cemetery
1972	12-Sep	Loretta McNamara Bartolomeo Died	Baltimore	Most Holy Redeemer Cemetery
1973	8-Oct	Casper (Gaspare Bartolomeo) Lawrence Died	Cleveland, OH	Fairview General Hospital

1977	26-Oct	Louis (Janni) Yanni Died	Bayonne, NJ	Holy Redeemer Cemetery, Jersey City, NJ
1982	Mar	Cecilia Bradbury Lawrence Died	Wheeling, WV	Two sons, Donald and Robert
1983	19-Nov	George (Giuseppe) Joseph Bartolomeo Died	Baltimore	Most Holy Redeemer Cemetery
1991	29-Oct	Florence Bartolomeo Yanni Died	New York	Unknown Cemetery
1994	22-Feb	Anna Bartolomeo Pfeifer Died	Peachtree City, GA	Most Holy Redeemer Cemetery
1999	16-Aug	Marjorie Decker Bartolomeo Died	Baltimore	Most Holy Redeemer Cemetery

Geographic Locations and Addresses Referenced in This Book

ITALY AND MEDITERRANEAN

Via Della Grazie – Torre de' Passeri, Italy, address of Santa Maria delle Grazie Church

Torre de' Passeri, Italy – Village from which the di Bartolomeos emigrated

Via San Vittorino – Location of di Bartolomeo home in Torre de' Passeri

Via San Vittorino – Torre de' Passeri, Italy. Earliest known address for Giovanni and Rosaria

Via San Vittorino – Torre de' Passeri, Italy. Birthplace of Maria, Gaspare, Luigi

Abruzzo/Abruzzi – Correct name is Abruzzo, Abruzzi was used based on early history of the regions known as the Abruzzis

Pescara –Major city in Abruzzo

Termoli – Train station on way to Naples

Foggio – Train station on way to Naples

Benevento – Train station on way to Naples

Caserta – Train station on way to Naples

Naples – Port city for departures to America

Bolognano, Italy – Town one and a half miles outside of Torre de' Passeri, where several ancestors lived

Chieti, Italy – Town 10 miles outside of Torre de' Passeri, where several ancestors were born

NEW YORK AND NEW YORK HARBOR

Hoffman Island – Quarantine island for entrance to Ellis Island

Swinburne Island – Quarantine island for entrance to Ellis Island

Ellis Island – Arrival and Immigration Center

509 Baltic Street Brooklyn, New York – First known U.S. address for Giovanni

Gowanus Canal – Industrial area of Brooklyn, NY, where Giovanni first resided in the U.S.

NEW JERSEY

492 Bramhall Avenue Jersey City, NJ – St. Patrick Roman Catholic Church

Union Street, Jersey City, NJ – Location of #14 Elementary School

Crescent Avenue and Astor Place – Location of PS #12 school

344 6th Street Jersey City, NJ – Holy Rosary Church

157 ½ Jackson Avenue, Jersey City, NJ – First U.S. home for di Bartolomeo family

54 Harrison Avenue, NJ – Second U.S. home for di Bartolomeo family

866 Broadway, Jersey City, NJ – Location of Louis and Florence Yanni barbershop

PENNSYLVANIA

St. Mary's Convent, Philadelphia – Maria Bartolomeo, a.k.a. Sister M. Siegberta

BALTIMORE AND MARYLAND

1301 Eastern Avenue, Baltimore, MD – Location listed on Giovanni's Declaration of Intent, January 1906

1400 Riverside Drive, Baltimore, MD, St. Mary, Star of the Sea – U.S. church for di Bartolomeo family

1400 Riverside Drive, Baltimore, MD, St. Mary, Star of the Sea – Sacrament of Confirmation Location for Anna, George, and Albert

107 West McComas Street, Baltimore, MD – First known address for di Bartolomeo family in Baltimore

Fort Avenue, Baltimore, MD – Second known residence of Giovanni and Rosaria in Baltimore

Camp Meade – Location where Gaspare taught Morse code during WWI

1501 South Charles Street, Baltimore, MD – Third known di Bartolomeo family residence in Baltimore

2763 Fenwick Avenue, Baltimore, MD – Last residence of Giovanni and Rosaria

1617 East 24th Street, Baltimore – First home of Anna and August Pfeifer

Centre and Howard Streets, Baltimore, MD – Baltimore City College

1333 Gorsuch Avenue, Baltimore, MD – George and Marjorie Bartolomeo residence

3602 Woodlea Avenue, Baltimore, MD – George and Marjorie Bartolomeo residence

Locust Point, Port Center of Baltimore – Area of first home location in Baltimore for di Bartolomeo

Sparrows Point – Industrial center of Baltimore

Federal Hill – Historic area of Baltimore, area of third home location in Baltimore for di Bartolomeo

115 Annapolis Boulevard, Brooklyn Park, MD – Location of Louis and Julia's home

809 Eager Street, Baltimore, MD – Albert and Loretta's home

4908 Arabia Avenue, Baltimore, MD – Albert and Loretta's home, 1930

Betterton Beach – Eastern Shore of Maryland Resort

Tolchester Beach – Eastern Shore of Maryland Resort

Magothy River – Summer home of George and Marjorie Bartolomeo

Brandon Shores – Location of Louis and Julia's first shore house

Orchard Beach – Summer home of Louis and Julia Bartolomeo

Ocean City, MD – A vacation destination replacing Betterton Beach

WASHINGTON, DC

15 H Street NE, Washington, DC – Address for Tony and Filomena di Nicolantonio Varrasso

3200 10th Street, NE, Washington, DC – Address for Tony and Filomena di Nicolantonio Varrasso

Arlington National Cemetery – Interment for Filomena and Tony Varrasso

WHEELING, WEST VIRGINIA

54 Lynwood Avenue, Wheeling, WV – Caspar [sic] Bartholomew Lawrence Form SS-5 U.S. Treasury Department

84 12th Street, Wheeling, WV – Casper and Cecelia Lawrence's residence

25 Locust Ave., Wheeling, WV – Casper and Cecelia Lawrence's residence

St. Joseph's Cathederal – Marriage of Casper and Cecelia in Wheeling, WV

Sources of Photographs, Graphics and Maps used in This Book

Page 9	Family photograph, courtesy of Bartolomeo family
Page 20	Torre de' Passeri landscape, Shutterstock.com 668489107 under license #3155169
Page 37	Church in Torre de' Passeri – Courtesy of Italianside.com; Domenico 2-19-2022
Page 40	Map of Italian railroad route – Wiki Commons.org; Free Media Repository
Page 44	Map of Giovanni's journey from Torre de Passeri to Port of Naples – Nat Case, INCase LLC.
Page 45	Italian Steam Engine – Unknown author, Wiki Media Commons; The Free Media Repository
Page 47	Port of Naples – Circa 1865, Wiki Media Commons, The Free Media Repository; George Summer
Page 49	Steamship – French Steam Sailor Cachemire; License Image 31863854(#4394425) Pixels.com
Page 54	Map of Giovanni's journey from Port of Naples through Mediterranean Sea – Nat Case, INCase LLC.
Page 55	Map of Giovanni's journey into New York Harbor, Ellis Island, Brooklyn and Jersey City
Page 56	Statue of Liberty – NPS.gov Ellis Island History and Culture, Statue of Liberty.org
Page 57	Hoffman Island – Photo courtesy of The New York Municipal Library
Page 58	Ellis Island – Photo courtesy of Statueofliberty.org
Page 60	Ellis Island Money Exchange – Photo courtesy of The New York Public Library
Page 62	Gowanus Canal – Courtesy of Brooklyn Public Library
Page 65	Steamship Werra – Courtesy estate of Michael Anuta, Ships of Our Ancestors 1993, Menominee, MI
Page 69	New Jersey Central Railroad Station – Shutterstock, Licensed user #315516927
Page 71	Church of the Holy Rosary Interior– Photo courtesy of Holy Rosary Church, Jersey City, New Jersey

Page 72	The Marylander – Courtesy of Wikipedia Fair Use, Steam, Steel, and Limited, Wm W. Kratville 1962
Page 79	Locust Point Jeffery Sauers – Courtesy of Jeffery Sauers; cpiproductions.com
Page 84	Shoemakers Tools - Shutterstock, Licensed user #315516927
Page 92	1912 Titanic Newsboy – Courtesy of Paul Van Scott. Pixels.com
Page 94	Albert and Louis Bartolomeo eating watermelon – Courtesy of Thomas and Donna Bartolomeo
Page 95	Fish and crab market – Courtesy of Damye Hahn; Faidley's Seafood, Baltimore, Maryland
Page 98	Louis Vicari Fruit Merchants – Courtesy of Ghosts of Baltimore
Page 102	Church of the Holy Rosary Exterior -Courtesy of Holy Rosary Church
Page 103	St. Mary, Star of the Sea – Courtesy DBpedia; creative commons; Share alike 3.0, unreported license
Page 104	St. Patrick Church – Courtesy St. Patrick Church
Page 105	St. Mary, Star of the Sea Exterior – Courtesy Catholic Diocese of Baltimore
Page 107	Rose Bartolomeo Brown First Communion – Courtesy of Anna Bartolomeo
Page 108	First Communion Mass – Shutterstock, Licensed user ID# 1405972268
Page 110	Manresa – Courtesy of Anna Bartolomeo
Page 111	St. Bernard's Athletics – Courtesy of G. Joseph Bartolomeo
Page 113	Maria Bartolomeo – Courtesy of Anna Bartolomeo
Page 116	Wright Aero Plane College Park, MD – collegeparkmd.gov
Page 118	George Bartolomeo on Ford – Courtesy of G. Joseph Bartolomeo
Page 119	1501 South Charles Street – Courtesy of Zillow.com
Page 121	Cleaning Marble Steps – Courtesy of A. Aubrey Bodine, Baltimore photographer, under licensed use.
Page 126	Julia and Louis Bartolomeo – Courtesy of Anna Bartolomeo
Page 127	Family at an outdoor picnic table – Courtesy of Anna Bartolomeo
Page 129	Louis, Julia, and children swimming – Courtesy of Anna Bartolomeo
Page 131	Louis Bartolomeo singing at the shore – Courtesy of Anna Bartolomeo
Page 133	Anna Bartolomeo Pfeifer -Courtesy Anna Bartolomeo
Page 141	Catholic Northwest Progress – Newspapers.com
Page 143	Casper and Cecelia Lawrence – Courtesy of Anna Bartolomeo
Page 144	Recruits at Camp Meade – history.army.mil, Camp Meade, MD, The WWI Era
Page 147	George Bartolomeo – G. Joseph Bartolomeo
Page 150	Baltimore City College exterior, Maryland Department –Enoch Pratt Free Library
Page 152	Baltimore City Class Room – Class picture George Bartolomeo

Page 154 Marjorie and George Bartolomeo – G. Joseph Bartolomeo

Page 155 Richard, Marjorie, Joe, George – G. Joseph Bartolomeo

Page 158 St. Bernard's Holy Name – Courtesy of George Bartolomeo

Page 159 Marjorie Bartolomeo in swimsuit – Courtesy of G. Joseph Bartolomeo

Page 161 Albert Bartolomeo – Courtesy of Thomas and Donna Bartolomeo

Page 161 Loretta and Albert Bartolomeo – Courtesy of Thomas and Donna Bartolomeo

Page 163 Loretta, Tom, and Albert – Courtesy of Thomas and Donna Bartolomeo

Page 164 Albert Bartolomeo Cheese Club – Courtesy of Thomas and Donna Bartolomeo

Page 167 Arundel Boat Club Pin – Courtesy of Thomas and Donna Bartolomeo

Page 167 Albert Bartolomeo Golfing – Courtesy of Thomas and Donna Bartolomeo

Page 169 Florence Bartolomeo Yanni – Courtesy of Anna Bartolomeo

Page 171 Louis Yanni – Courtesy of Anna Bartolomeo

Page 173 Wall Street crash headline – businessinsider.com, Pixels.com, Pinterest

Page 177 Sheppard Stove Company advertisement – Newspaper ad, *Baltimore Sun* newspaper

Page 178 Map of di Bartolomeo's Baltimore residences and points of interest – Nat Case, INCase LLC.

Page 183 George Bartolomeo playing violin – Courtesy of G. Joseph Bartolomeo

Page 187 Walther Gardens Snowball Stand – Courtesy of Walther Gardens, Baltimore; Matthew Wittek

Page 189 Marjorie on Day sailor – Courtesy of G. Joseph Bartolomeo

Page 190 Louise – Courtesy of Internet Archive, Free Books, Sidewheel Steamers of the Chesapeake Bay, 1948

Page 191 George and Albert Bartolomeo -Courtesy Thomas and Donna Bartolomeo

Page 192 Louis, John Bartolomeo and Family dog -Courtesy Anna Bartolomeo

Page 194 Charles Austin and Joe Bartolomeo – Courtesy of G. Joseph Bartolomeo

Page 195 George Bartolomeo on the boat dock at Magothy River – Courtesy of Carolynn S. Bartolomeo

Page 196 Dick Bartolomeo and Pop Decker – Courtesy of Dick Bartolomeo

Endnotes and Source Citations

1 1838-1847 Allegati to Marriages of Torre de' Passeri, Pescara, Italia (FHL#1536496)
2 1838-1847 Civil Birth, Marriage and Death Records of Torre de' Passeri, Pescara, Italia (FHL#1355683)
3 wikipedia.org., Abbey of Casauria
4 christianity.com/church/historytimeline
5 Italian Side, Genealogy in Torre de' Passeri
6 European Route of Industrial Heritage, On the Industrial Heritage of Italy
7 1809-1814 Civil Birth, Marriage and Death Records of Torre de' Passeri, Pescara, Italia (FHL#1331952)
8 1857 Civil Birth, Marriage and Death Records of Torre de' Passeri, Pescara, Italia (FHL#1355685)
9 Torre de' Passeri, Pescara, Italia, Marriages #2016413, Family History Library, atti#18 in 1888 Marriages
10 1866-1910 Civil Marriage Records of Torre de' Passeri, Pescara, Italia (FHL#2016413)
11 1865 Civil Birth, Marriage and Death Records of Torre de' Passeri, Pescara, Italia (FHL#1355686)
12 1865 Civil Birth, Marriage and Death Records of Torre de' Passeri, Pescara, Italia (FHL#1355686)
13 1857-65 Civil Allegati for the Marriages of TDP, Pescara, Italia, (FHL#1536498)
14 1837-1847 Allegati to Marriages of Torre de' Passeri, Pescara, Italia, Genealogical Society of Utah (FHL#1536496)
15 1838-1847 Civil Birth, Marriage and Death Records of Torre de' Passeri, Pescara, Italia, (FHL#1355683)
16 1849 Civil Birth, Marriage and Death Records of Torre de' Passeri, Pescara, Italia (FHL#1536496) #38
17 Ellis Island Immigration Center
18 history.com/new/steerage-act-immigration-19th-century
19 history.com/new/steerage-act-immigration-19th-century
20 Ellis Island National Monument, The Immigrant Journey, 2008-2013, APN Media, LLC
21 Santos v. The Cachemire, 38F.518 (1889) Case Law Access Project
22 Diocese Pescara, Italia

23 New York, U.S. Arriving Passenger and Crew List, August 21, 1893, Cachemire
24 History of Railroads in Italy
25 History of Naples pg. xlvi, University of Virginia, 1890, K. Baedeker
26 Santos v. The Cachemire, 38F.518 (1889) Case Law Access Project
27 *New York Times*, August 20, 1893
28 *New York Times*, August 20, 1893
29 New York, U.S. Arriving Passenger and Crew List, August 21, 1893, Cachemire
30 *New York Times*, August 25, 1893
31 *New York Times*, August 25, 1893
32 History of New York Cities Swinburne and Hoffman Islands
33 *Smithsonian Magazine*, January 6, 2010
34 museumoffamilyhistory.com/imm-hai-trachoma.htm
35 New York, U.S. Arriving Passenger and Crew List, August 21, 1893, Cachemire
36 oldskyscrapers.org, Skyline, 1900-1916
37 U.S. Naturalization Records, City Court, Brooklyn, V59 R404, October 18, 1893
38 Gowanus Canal History, gowanuscanal.org
39 U.S. Federal Census Hudson, 6th Precinct, 7th Ward, Jersey City and U.S. Cities Directory, Jersey City, NJ 1898 pg. 24
40 New York U.S. Arriving Passenger and Crew List, January 12, 1897, Werra, pg. 1
41 St. Patrick Catholic Church Baptisms Register for Anna di Bartolomeo, March 24, 1898, pg. 353
42 1867-1888 Civil Marriage Allegati for Torre de' Passeri, Pescara, Italia, (FHL#2016601)
43 1866-1900 Civil Birth Records for Torre de' Passeri, Pescara, Italia (FHL#2016412)
44 1866-1900 Civil Birth Records for Torre de' Passeri, Pescara, Italia (FHL#2016412)
45 New York U.S. Arriving Passenger and Crew List, January 12, 1897 Werra, pg. 1
46 New York U.S. Arriving Passenger and Crew List, January 12, 1897 Werra, pg. 1
47 history.com/news/post-office
48 projects.leadr.msu.edu/
49 postalmuseums.si.edu
50 New Jersey Births and Christening Index, 1660-1931 (FHL Film #4209857)
51 New Jersey Births and Christening Index, 1660-1931 (FHL Film #4909860)
52 United States World War II Draft Registration, 19401947 #10714, Serial no. 1449
53 United States Social Security Application and Claims, November 30, 1972, #05244711
54 reference.com/history/cost/1900 April 12, 2020
55 1910 United States Federal Census, Dept. of Commerce Baltimore Ward 23, District 3, April 21/22, 1910

56 britannica.com, Baltimore and Ohio Railroad, B&O Railroad Museum

57 U.S. Cities Directories, NJ Jersey City, pg. 25, December 28, 1905

58 Department of Commerce 13th Census of the United States, April 21-22, Baltimore, Maryland

59 New York U.S. Passenger and Crew List, April 7, 1896, pg. 52, Kaiser Wilhelm

60 *Washington Evening Star*, August 9, 1906, pg. 16

61 Quartermaster General U.S. Spanish American War Index and U.S. National Cemetery Interment

62 *The Washington Post,* August 1, 1906, pg. 4

63 1865 Civil Birth, Marriage and Death Records, Torre de' Passeri, Pescara, Italia (FHL # 1355686)

64 U.S. Civil War Pension Index, Washington, D.C., R #10170, 1861-1934

65 Washington, D.C., U.S. Select Death Burial Index, #176901950 (FHL#2116109) Ref # 330388

66 United States National Cemetery Interment Control Form, Marker Ordered March 3, 1930

67 Department of Commerce 13th Census of the United States, April 21-22, Baltimore, Maryland

68 Baltimore City, The History of Baltimore, pgs. 9-16

69 britannica.com, Johns Hopkins, American Philanthropist, December 20, 1921

70 Andrew Carnegie, The Gospel of Wealth

71 history.com, The Great Baltimore Fire, This Day in History, March 7, 1904

72 Conversation with George Bartolomeo, 1974

73 Sanborn Fire Insurance Maps, Baltimore County, Baltimore City, 1914-1951, pg. 401, image 104

74 *Baltimore Sun,* January 20, 1916

75 Bethlehem Steel Corporate Archives, LebTown, September 15, 2018

76 United States Census, Maryland, Baltimore, Ward 23, April 22-23, 1910

77 United States Federal Census, April 21 and 22, 1910, Maryland, Baltimore, Ward 23

78 Recorded Interview with Anna Pfeifer Bartolomeo, March 1984

79 Recorded Interview with Anna Pfeifer Bartolomeo, March 1984

80 Recorded Interview with Anna Pfeifer Bartolomeo, March 1984

81 Interview with George Bartolomeo, 1974

82 Recorded Interview with Anna Pfeifer Bartolomeo, March 1984

83 capturedandexposed.com/theblackhandinbaltimore

84 Recorded Interview with Anna Pfeifer Bartolomeo, March 1984

85 Education, Maryland State Archives, State Department of Education, September 29, 2015

86 How America Graduated from High School Ed., 1910-1960, Claudia Goldin, Dept. of Econ., Harvard University

87 Recorded Interview with Anna Bartolomeo Pfeifer, 1982

88 nationalbohemian.com/history/default.aspx

89 Interview with George Bartolomeo, 1972

90 Interview with George Bartolomeo, 1972

91 Congregation of St. Joseph 2022, CSJoseph.org

92 Recorded interview with Anna Pfeifer Bartolomeo, March 1984

93 St. Patrick Roman Catholic Church, Jersey City, NJ, April 24, 1888, pg. 353

94 Chiesa Italiana Del Santissimo, Rosario Certificate of Baptism, May 7, 1899

95 Holy Rosary Church, Jersey City, New Jersey; Christina Szpala, Holy Rosary Archive Search, January 12, 2022

96 Baltimore Roman Catholic Parish Baptisms, 1782-1919, St. Leo's Registry, 20 June 1909, pg. 214, entry 2

97 Baltimore Roman Catholic Parish Baptisms, 1782-1919, St. Leo's Registry, 20 June 1909, pg. 214, entry 2

98 Interview with Anna Bartolomeo Pfeifer, 1984. No school records have been located for St. Mary, Star of the Sea

99 Baltimore Roman Catholic Parish Congregational Records

100 Baltimore Roman Catholic Parish Congregational Records

101 Jesuit Online Library, St. Ignatius and St. Mary's County, June 1, 1931

102 Baltimore Chapter of The Grand Knights, Chapter History

103 The Sisters of St. Francis, Personal Letter from Sister Andrew Pershing, Congregational Archivist, June 22, 2001

104 The Sisters of St. Francis, Personal Letter from Sister Andrew Pershing, Congregational Archivist, June 22, 2001

105 whitehouse.gov/thepresidents

106 Catholicism and American Freedom, John T. McGreevy, 2003

107 boundarystones.weta.org, August 26, 2015

108 United States Federal Census, Maryland, Baltimore, Ward 23, District 3, January 13, 1920

109 Anatomy of a Baltimore Row House, baltimoreheritage.org

110 Geo. Science World, Cockeysville Marble, A Heritage Stone from Maryland, October 21, 1920

111 baltimore.org/anatomyofabaltimorerowhouse

112 United States Federal Census, Maryland, Anne Arundel, Brooklyn Park, 5th District, January 7, 1920

113 Declaration of Intention for Naturalization, March 3, 1915

114 United States Federal Census, Maryland, Anne Arundel, Brooklyn Park, 5th District, January 7, 1920

115 St. Mary, Star of the Sea Marriage Register, June 13, 1915, pg. 194, Reel M-2710

116 United States WWI Draft Registration, 19-1-23A, June 5, 1917

117 United States WWI Draft Registration, 19-1-23A, June 5, 1917

118 United States WWI Draft Registration, 19-1-23A, June 5, 1917

119 United States WWII Draft Registration, 1942 Board #5, Serial no. 1670, Baltimore County

120 United States of America Certificate of Naturalization no. 6483004, September 10, 1945

121 Virginia Bureau of Vital Statistics Marriage Registers, 1853-1935, Virginia State Archives

122 Recorded Interview with Anna Bartolomeo Pfeifer, 1984

123 United States Federal Census, Maryland, Baltimore, Ward 9, District 0139, January 15, 1920

124 State of Maryland Certificate of Death, District 25#12892. Filed December 27, 1922. Charles Brooke, MD.

125 United States Federal Census, Maryland, Baltimore, District 0490, April 8, 1930

126 Immigration History 2019, Emergency Quota Law 1921, University of Texas at Austin

127 Deville, John, Italians in The U.S., Catholic Encyclopedia vol. 8 NY 16, January 2022

128 Seattle Civil Rights Labor History Project, University of Washington, Kristen Dimick

129 *The New York Times*, August 6, 2000, Section A, pg. 4; Timothy Egan

130 history.com, news, KKK-terror-during-prohibition; Becky Little, January 15, 2019

131 One Hundred Percent American: The Rebirth and Decline, the KKK in the 1920s, Thomas R. Pegram, Loyola Univ.

132 1866-1900 Civil Birth Records of Torre de' Passeri, Pescara, Italia (Microfilm #2016412)

133 Interview with Anna Bartolomeo Pfeifer, 1984

134 United States Treasury Dept. Form SS-5, Internal Revenue, November 27, 1936

135 United States Treasury Dept. Form SS-5, Internal Revenue, November 27, 1936

136 United States Federal Census, West Virginia, Ohio, Wheeling, Triadelphia County, April 12, 1940

137 Interview with Thomas Bartolomeo and Lynn Bartolomeo

138 On the physical Baptismal certificate, George struck through Feb. 23 and wrote Feb. 22, midnight

139 United States World War II Draft Registration Order #12133, Serial no. 2578, 1942

140 Interview with George Bartolomeo, 1974

141 baltimoreheritage.org, Baltimore City College History, History of Ed. in Maryland

142 Baltimore City College Alumni Association, Notable Knights of Baltimore City College

143 United States WWI Draft Registration, Serial no. 1105/Order #A106, September 12, 1918

144 United States WWI Draft Registration, Serial no. 1105/Order #A1060, 1918

145 United States WWI Draft Registration, Serial no. 1105/Order #A1060, 1918

146 U.S. Cities Directories, Maryland, Baltimore, 1929, pg. 244

147 United States Federal Census, Maryland, Baltimore, Ward 9, April 2, 1940

148 Marriage Certificate, Associated Archives of Baltimore Diocese, August 29, 1927

149 Office Registrar of Vital Statistics, Board of Health, Baltimore, Maryland, #A12937

150 United States Federal Census, Maryland, Baltimore, Ward 27, D3, January 19/20, 1920

151 United States Federal Census, Maryland, Baltimore, Ward 27 April 10, 1940

152 United States Federal Census, Maryland, Baltimore, Ward 9, District 4, April 2, 1930

153 United States Public Records Index; Form 214 Report of Separation from United States Marine Corp

154 Interview with George Bartolomeo, 1974

155 St. Bernard's Holy Name News Vol. 4, No. 2, February 1947

156 U.S. Cities Directories, Maryland, Baltimore, 1956, Resided on Gorsuch Ave. 1954 (Joe Bartolomeo USMC Records)

157 United States Federal Census, Maryland, Baltimore, Ward 23, January 13, 1920

158 U.S. Cities Directories Baltimore, Maryland, 1920, pg. 323

159 U.S. Cities Directories Baltimore, Maryland, 1929, pg. 244

160 American Law Reports V3 1919, Jones Hollow Ware Company v. Crane

161 *The Baltimore Sun,* June 26, 1928, pg. 6

162 United States Department of Commerce, U.S. Federal Census, Maryland, Baltimore, Ward 10, April 22, 1910

163 Provided by Thomas Bartolomeo, December 1, 2021

164 United States Federal Census, Maryland, Baltimore City, April 10, 1930

165 United States WWII Draft Registration, Serial no. #1449, Order #10714, 1941

166 U.S. Cities Directories, 1956, pg. 106

167 Provided by Thomas Bartolomeo, with photograph of his father Albert holding club plaque

168 United States Federal Census, Maryland, Baltimore City, Sheet 8B, April 5, 1930

169 *Baltimore Sun*, May 25, 1919, pg. 57

170 State of Maryland, Bureau of Vital Statistics, Maryland State Archives, 1914-1940

171 Jersey Journal, pg. 12, Wednesday July 24, 1928

172 United States Federal Census, New Jersey, Hudson, Bayonne, April 8, 1940

173 Church of The Holy Rosary Baptismal Certificate, May 1899, Reverend H. Federici

174 Baltimore City Directory, 1928, pg. 743

175 United States Federal Census, April 2, 1930

176 United States Federal Census, Maryland, Baltimore, Ward 9, District 4, April 2, 1930

177 Fraser – Fed. Reserve Wages and Hours of Labor, Boot and Shoe Making Ind. 1910-1932, Bulletin No. 579

178 Recorded interview with Anna Pfeifer Bartolomeo, March 1984

179 Personal Site Visit, 1957-1975; for Woodlea Avenue Property Description

180 Personal Site Visit, 1957-1975; for Woodlea Avenue Property Description

181 Certificate of Death, Health Department, City of Baltimore, #8329156, November 14, 1983

182 Certificate of Death, State of Maryland, Department of Health, issued August 17, 1999

183 Side-wheel Steamers of the Chesapeake Bay, 1800-1947, Hain, John

184 Recorded interview with Anna Pfeifer Bartolomeo, March 1984

185 The only records that were available documenting high school completion are for George and Florence

186 Interview with Thomas Bartolomeo, November 2021

187 Certificate of Death, Health Department, City of Baltimore, F31260, January 15, 1937, 5:10 p.m.

188 Baltimore City Death Certificates, Giovanni – F31260, January 16, 1937; Rosaria – E51782, November 5, 1938

SOURCE NOTES

Sources Used for This Book

abruzzogeneaology.org

Allegati to Marriages Torre de' Passeri 1837-1847

American Waltham Watch Company Archives

Anatomy of a Baltimore Row Home

Associated Archives at St. Mary's Seminary and University

A Stove Less Ordinary Blog, Howell Harris, January 24, 2018

Baltimore City Directories

Baltimore Roman Catholic Parish Congregational Records

Baltimore City College Archives

Baltimore City Government Records

Baltimore Magazine

Baltimore Sun, January 20, 1916

Baltimore Sun, June 26, 1928

Baltimore Sun, December 11, 1929

Baltimore Sun, May 30, 1934

Baltimore Sun, "Getting an Oyster Down Pat," February 12, 1998

Bartlett-Hayward Company

Bethlehem Steel Corp. Archives

catholicexchange.com

catholicculture.org

Cincinnati Enquirer, July 8, 1923

Civil Birth Records of Torre de' Passeri, Pescara, Italy, 1866-1900

Civil Marriage Records of Torre de' Passeri, Pescara, Italy, 1866-1910

1858 Civil Births Torre de' Passeri, Pescara, Italia (FHL#1355685)

1888 Civil Marriages Torre de' Passeri, Pescara, Italia (FHL#2016413)

1888 Torre de' Passeri, Pescara, Italia (FHL#2016601)

1889 Torre de' Passeri, Pescara, Italia (FHL#2016412)

1891 Torre de' Passeri, Pescara, Italia (FHL#2016412)

1894 Torre de' Passeri, Pescara, Italia (FHL#2016412)

1867-1888 Civil Marriages Allegati for Torre de' Passeri, Pescara, Italia (FHL#2016601)

1865 Civil Births, Marriages and Deaths, Torre de' Passeri, Pescara, Italia (FHL#1355686)

1848-1865 Civil Births, Marriages and Deaths, Torre de' Passeri, Pescara, Italia (FHL#1355684)

1857-1864 Civil Births, Marriages and Deaths, Torre de' Passeri, Pescara, Italia (FHL#1355685)

1838-1847 Civil Births, Marriages and Deaths, Torre de' Passeri, Pescara, Italia (FHL#1355683)

1837-1847 Allegati to Marriages of Torre de' Passeri, Pescara, Italia (FHL#1536496)

1857-1865 Civil Allegati for Marriages of Torre de' Passeri, Pescara, Italia (FHL#1536498)

1866-1910 Civil Marriages of Torre de' Passeri, Pescara, Italia (FHL#2016413)

Chesapeake Bay Program Sciences

Congregational Archivist, The Sisters of St. Francis of Philadelphia

Cross Street Market History Archive

Ellis Island Immigration Center

Evening Sun July 30, 1963

Family History Library, Salt Lake City, Utah

findagrave.com

Food and Culture, Natash Lavender, 2019

Genealogy in Torre de' Passeri

Gen Tracer – Kathy Kilpatrick

Harvard University Press, The Organization of the Shoe and Boot Industry; (Cornell)

History of Railroads in Italy

History of NYC's Swinburne and Hoffman Islands

Interview with Anna Bartolomeo Pfeifer, 1984

Interview with Thomas Bartolomeo, 2021

Loyola High School Year Book

localhistories.org

Maryland Historical Society

Maryland Federal Naturalization Records

moosmossis.org

New Jersey Births and Christening Index, 1660-1931

New York Times; Time Machine

New York Times, The Charm City of H.L. Mencken September 4, 1988

New York, U.S. Arriving Passengers and Crew List (Including Castle Garden and Ellis Island) 1820-1957)

North German Lloyd Passengers List

Ohio Death Records, 1938-2007 Cert# 075253

oldskyscapers.org

Pennsylvania Death Certificates, 1906-1963

Pescara Italy State Archives

Pittsburgh Press, July 1, 1923

Public Health Report, Ship Sanitary Conditions, 1892-93

Pubblicazioni di Matrimonio, Tipi dei sed Retari Comunali, Treviso, 1888

St. Mary, Star of the Sea, Marriage Registration

Santos v. The Cachemire, 38F.518 (1889), Case Law Access Project

St. Bernard Roman Catholic Church Holy Name Society Publications

Side Wheel Steamers of the Chesapeake Bay, 1880-1947, Hain, John

Site visits: 1501 South Charles Street, Church of the Holy Rosary, St. Mary, Star of the Sea

Smithsonian Magazine

State of Maryland Land Records

statistica.com

Torre de' Passeri Marriage Records

Torre de' Passeri, Italy, Pescara Civil Archives

The Depression Era in Baltimore, December 3, 2009

U.S. Cities Directories, 1822-1995

U.S. Find a Grave Index, 1600-current

U.S. Federal State of Maryland Census, 1860-1940

U.S. Federal State of New Jersey Census, 1860-1940

U.S. Federal Census, State of West Virginia

U.S. Naturalization Records

U.S. Naturalization Record Index, 1791-1992

U.S. Quartermaster General; Washington, DC Report of Interment

U.S. Schools Year Books, 1900-1999

U.S. Social Security Applications and Claims, 1936-2007

U.S. Geological Surveys

U.S. World War I Draft Registration Cards

U.S. World War II Draft Registration Cards

U.S. WWII Hospital Admissions

U.S. Index to Public Records, 1994-2019

Washington, DC Select Deaths and Burials, 1769-1960

Washington Post, August 01, 1906

Weekly Abstract of Sanitation Reports, June 9, 1893, pg. 430